IT'S A LONG WAY
TO GUACAMOLE

THE TEX-MEX COOKBOOK

IT'S A LONG WAY TO GUACAMOLE

The Tex-Mex Cookbook

by Ann Worley &
Rue Judd

Original written by
Ann Worley and Rue Judd
Revised by
Ann Worley and Margaret Jones
Drawings by Marti Patchell, Margaret Jones and Sarah Vickers
Cover painting: Donna Josey

Library of Congress Cataloging-in-Publication Data
Card # 87-080795 ISBN: 0-9604842-3-X
J&W Tex Mex Publications

Published by: J&W Tex - Mex

It's a Long Way to Guacamole
The Tex-Mex Cookbook
www.annworley.com

Written by Ann Worley and Rue Judd
Revised in 2003 by friends, Ann Worley and Margaret Jones

Cover: painting by Donna Josey, design by Margaret Jones

First printing: 1978
Sixteenth printing: 2003

Printed in China

To wonderful friends, who made this book possible. Without them, there would be no book.

The inspiration for *It's a Long Way to Guacamole* grew over the years as we tried to assemble a collection of the favorite, tried-and-true recipes of our fellow *Tex-Mexican* food aficionados in and around Washington, DC. A number of years ago, several Texas couples, transplanted to the Washington area, began gathering on occasional Sunday evenings for informal Mexican suppers. The hostess would plan the menu and ask each couple to bring a specific dish. Over the years, the group has grown. Though some of its original members have returned to the Texas homeland, many others have arrived to take their places. Other members of the group are Texans by marriage; longing, envious Oklahomans and Louisianans; other Southwesterners; and even a few Yankees, but all enjoy *Tex-Mex* food.

It's a Long Way to Guacamole is a collection of recipes drawn from 'the group' and our Texas families. Our Mexican food is unabashedly *Tex-Mex*, the food of the northern Mexican provinces which has migrated so felicitously and deliciously across the border into and throughout Texas.

Today, the Mexican influence and cooking tastes in the USA is on the rise. Accordingly, ingredients for cooking Mexican food are available in super-makets all over the country, not only in Texas and the Southwest.

Whether you wish a simple taco and chili supper with the family, a cooperative covered dish supper, an elegant and spicy brunch, or a festive dinner party, we hope *It's a Long Way to Guacamole* will enrich and enhance your culinary endeavors.

Many have referred to *It's a Long Way to Guacamole* as the underground bestseller. When first published, our funds were limited and therefore, our pages were tight and our marketing was regional. Our first attempt (5,000 books) was to look like an avocado skin, but actually, in final form, it looked like a hymnal...... not exactly our idea, but it sold! Twenty-five years have gone by, and this little book, which was easily tucked into a purse for a trip to the grocery store, has now evolved into a book that requires a grocery list!

Table of Contents

Notes

Appetizers

Notes

Soups & Chili

Salads

Notes

Egg Dishes

Main Dishes

Notes

Vegetables & Side Dishes

Breads

Notes

Desserts

The Basics

Basic Techniques, Ingredients, Sauces & Fillings

Mexican food originated with the Aztecs. Tortillas
and tamales were being consumed with gusto
long before Columbus discovered the 'New
World'. The basics are still the same: corn, beans,
chiles, tomatoes and avocados - all New World
products, natural and largely unprocessed foods.
The Spanish added olive oil, wheat flour, wine
and some cooking variations, but these additions
invariably incorporated the local ingredients.
Texans have further modified this delicious food
to give it its unique *Tex-Mex* flavor.

Tortillas

Tortillas (tor-tee-yas) are the thin, round, unleavened
pancakes made of 'masa', a coarsely ground corn
flour or finely ground corn meal. Tortillas are - liter-
ally - at the bottom of *Tex-Mex* food - also around,
in or with! The versatile and essential tortilla may be
served fresh and hot from the griddle, or fried crisp,
and used as an edible 'plate' to be covered with other
delicacies (chalupas). Tortillas are used in tacos, as a
crisp wrapper, for tostados as a chip, and as a rolled
pancake in enchiladas, or as a 'pasta' in chilaquiles.

22

Tortillas are available as follows:

Fresh, frozen, or pre-fried, these tortillas have been cooked but need reheating or frying to serve. At some Mexican restaurants fresh tortillas made daily may be purchased by the dozen - telephone first! Tortillas can be made in your kitchen - a great activity with or without children!

Freshly cooked tortillas straight from your griddle with butter and a sprinkle of salt will make you an addict! Crisp fried tortillas from a good restaurant are hard to beat for convenience when many are needed (as for a party); however, for soft tortillas, the home-made handmade variety is by far the best.

Soft Tortillas

Masa Harina by Quaker is available in most large
supermarkets and always in Latin American
groceries. (Caution! Regular cornmeal is not the
same and will not work!)

2 cups Masa Harina
1 cup water

Mix masa and water with a fork or your hands,
blending well for a couple of minutes. Dough
should hold together; if not, add a little more
water, a tablespoon at a time. Shape into 12 to
16 balls and cover bowl to prevent drying. Allow to stand for 15 to 20 minutes. Flatten each
ball of dough with tortilla press or rolling pin to
form 6-inch circles.

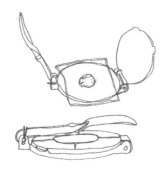

A relatively inexpensive tortilla press is available at
most cookware stores, kitchen bazaars or major
department stores; it makes tortilla production
a total snap! Cut one plastic clear sandwich bag
apart to form two squares. Place a ball of masa
dough between the plastic in the tortilla press.
Press down hard with the handle, remove the
flattened dough, and gently peel away the plastic
sheets, one side at a time. Place the tortilla on
an ungreased hot griddle or iron skillet and cook
approximately one minute on each side. Remove
and place in a dishtowel or napkin to keep warm.
As one tortilla is cooking, press out another to
take its place. Children love to pile grated cheese
on the first cooked side of the tortilla to melt
while the second side is cooking.

The stack of tortillas may be served immediately or
kept warm for an hour or two. If they are served
after a longer period of time, wrap the stack in
foil and warm in a slow oven. These soft tortillas
may also be used at this point for Soft Tacos (see
Index)

Tortillas for Enchiladas

The fresh cooked corn tortillas (or frozen) are softened in oil before filling. Heat 1 inch of vegetable oil in a 10 inch skillet over medium high heat, or use deep fat fryer set at 350°. With tongs, dip the tortilla in the oil until it becomes limp; this takes only about 5 seconds. Drain on a paper towel, fill and roll, placing the flap side down in a casserole.

Crisp Fried Tortillas

Heat 1 inch of vegetable oil, shortening, or lard in a skillet over medium high heat (350°) or use deep fat fryer set at 350°. Fry the whole tortilla, turning once or twice, for about minute until crisp. Whole crisp tortillas are also called tostados or chalupa shells.

Taco shells are made by placing the tortilla in the hot oil and then folding as soon as they soften. Hold the edges about 1 inch apart with tongs and fry until crisp. This will take about a minute per shell.

FRIED CRISP FOR CHALUPAS

TACO SHELL

To make crisp tostado chips, cut the tortillas into quarters and fry until crisp, a handful at a time.

26

Tostado chips are used for spooning or dipping. For a different look, cut the tortilla into half-inch strips, using scissors. The crisp strips are good instead of crackers with soup. Serve Mexican Chicken Portuguese or Chiles Verdes con Carne (see Index) over these crisp strips with rice.

Soft Tacos

Heat a griddle to medium high temperature. Lightly brush one side of the tortilla with vegetable oil and place the oiled side down on the griddle and brush the other side with oil. Allow about 30 seconds cooking time per side. Remove tortillas as they cook and stack them between 2 folded dish towels to keep them warm or place them in a tortilla warmer. Place 2 tablespoons filling in each tortilla and fold. For soft chicken tacos use either Chicken , Tomatoes & Green Chiles or Seasoned Chicken. For soft beef tacos use Spiced Ground Beef (see Index) or leftover chili. Serve with any or all of the following: grated cheese, chopped tomatoes, chopped onion, shredded lettuce, salsa.

Beans

Beans are present in some form in almost every Mexican meal. In many Mexican households a pot of beans is always cooking. Beans are a valuable and inexpensive protein source and respond well to imagi-  native preparation. Versatile beans may be served as soon as cooked, refried, combined in sauces or used in other dishes. Pinto beans and black beans are the varieties most used in *Tex-Mex* cooking. Note: One cup of dried beans yields approximately 2½ cups of cooked beans. Cooked beans freeze well. Try freezing in 1½ cup quantities, using plastic sandwich bags.

Chiles

Chiles are peppers; fleshy fruits ranging from the tiny pea-sized chile pequin to the 8 inch Ana-heim green chile. Not all peppers are of the eye-watering hot variety; some are sweet and mild, while others are in between. The pepper plants, especially those of the small pepper are attractive garden or house plants. Commonly available peppers used for *Tex-Mex* cooking are:

Jalapeño: Dark green; 2 to 3 inches long; easy to grow in home gardens; sometimes available fresh in large markets hot; easily available canned and pickled whole or sliced.

Serrano: Dark, dark green (turns red as it gets very mature); ½ to ¾ inch in diameter; very hot; available fresh as well as both canned and pickled.

Green Chiles or Poblanos: Bright green; 5 to 6 inches long and 1½ to 2 inches in diameter at top; varies from mild to hot; often available fresh; always available canned (labeled Whole Green Chiles), use for Chiles Relleños; also available chopped.

Chile Pequin: Tiny, pea sized bright dark green changing to bright red; extremely hot! Use with caution; rarely available fresh in markets, but easy to grow and makes an attractive garden plant; available dried.

Pimientos: Bright red, usually available canned, sweet and mild; also good for adding touches of color.

Pasilla: Very dark in color, with a strong, hot, pronounced flavor. Good for sauces and marinades.

Chipotle: Chipotle Peppers(Chee-pote-lays):Dark red and dried jalapeño peppers that have been dried slowly over smoke. Available dried or ready to use as 'Chipotle In Adobo' (available in cans). NOTE: When handling hot peppers, always wear rubber gloves!!

<u>Green Peppers</u>: Green, changing to red when mature on plant; very mild and sweet.

A number of the recipes call for canned "tomatoes and green chiles," which are stewed tomatoes with hot green peppers. Ro-Tel ® brand of tomatoes and green chiles have been dependably consistent in quality and degree of hotness.

Spices

Spices are all important to good *Tex-Mex* cooking. All the recipes described in this book incorporate spices that are readily available. Stock your shelves with.....

Cumin
Oregano
Cilantro
Chili powder

Chili powder is a blend of ground dried peppers, cumin and oregano. Commercial brands vary widely from mild to hot Mexican style. Find the one to suit your taste.
... and plant in your garden or in pots in your kitchen:
Parsley
Chervil (uncurly parsley)

Cilantro*
Oregano
Pepper plants

Should you have an excess of hot ripe peppers at summer's end, allow peppers to turn red on the plant. Then pick and string with a large needle on a cord for an interesting kitchen decoration. Use one by one all winter long or wire into a wreath for Christmas!

*To store fresh cilantro: place in a plastic bag and store in refrigerator or cut stems and place in a glass of water. Cover with plastic bag and store in refrigerator.

Avocados

There are two main kinds of avocados. The ones grown in Mexico and the Southwest have a heavy dark skin which becomes almost black as it ripens. These are pear-shaped, pear-sized fruits with a

seed the size of a large walnut. Avocados grown in Florida and the Caribbean have a thinner brighter green skin and a flesh with a higher water content. The fruit tends to be considerably larger with a seed the size of a lemon. Generally, one Florida avocado equals two California avocados in volume.

Avocado plants may be easily grown from the avocado seeds. Peel away the brown outer covering of the seed to expose the pale seed. With the pointed end up, stick 3 or 4 toothpicks into the seed to act as supports and place in a glass of water as shown. Keep water level high enough to cover the lower half of seed. The seed will sprout. Often sprouting takes as much as 4 to 6 weeks, so please be patient! When the sprout reaches a height of 3 to 4 inches, roots will also have appeared below the seed. Plant in a pot of good rich soil, just to barely cover the seed. Water every other day, as the soil should be moist. When the sprout reaches 6 inches above the soil, cut back to about 4 inches to promote branching. Continue to cut branches back to encourage further branching.

The avocado plants have beautiful large leaves and are decorative house trees. Be sure they have plenty of sunlight.

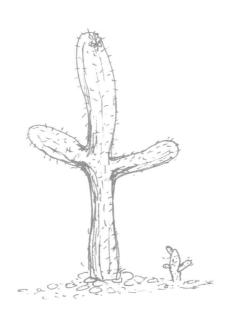

Sauces and Fillings

Tex-Mex food lends itself to so many variations, in
large part because the sauces or a filling can
change the character of a recipe, hence making
for so much versatility and creativity. We have
provided the reader with the basic sauces and the
basic fillings in this chapter. Bear in mind that
with the addition or omission of one or two ingredients, the sauce or filling takes on a new life.
Get to know some of these 'basics' and experi-
ment for your own enjoyment.

Hot Sauce (Salsa)

1   large onion, chopped
1   teaspoon vegetable oil or fresh bacon drippings
2   cups peeled ripe tomatoes, chopped (3 or 4)
3   jalapeño peppers (or more or less to taste) finely
       chopped
¼   teaspoon salt
1   clove garlic, crushed

Sauté onion in oil until softened. The pieces should
not be browned. Add tomatoes, peppers, salt and
garlic and simmer for 40 minutes to 1 hour, or
until thickened.

*Make this sauce with flavorful summer tomatoes and freeze for
wintertime use. When ripe tomatoes are not available, substitute two
10 ounce cans of tomatoes and green chiles and adjust the jalapeños.*

Salsa Fresca, Uncooked Hot Sauce

6   *large tomatoes*
1   *8 ounce can tomato sauce*
2-4 *jalapeño peppers, seeded and finely chopped*
1   *bunch green onions, minced (including crisp tops)*
1   *clove garlic minced (optional)*
    salt to taste
2   *tablespoons wine vinegar*
1   *tablespoons olive oil*

Peel and finely chop the tomatoes. Add the remaining ingredients and allow to sit several hours before serving.

Pico de Gallo

3   *medium tomatoes, peeled and chopped*
1   *medium onion, chopped*
1   *clove of garlic, minced*
3-4 *serrano or jalapeño chiles, seeded and chopped*
1   *lime, juiced*
    salt to taste
¼   *cup chopped fresh cilantro*

Combine ingredients and allow to sit at least one hour.

Note: Pico de Gallo also appears in the 'Salad' chapter with the addition of avocado.

36

Picante Sauce

½   cup jalapeños, finely chopped
1   cup red onions, finely chopped
1   cup tomatoes, finely chopped
¼   cup fresh lime juice
6   tablespoons fresh cilantro, finely chopped
2   tablespoons olive oil
     salt to taste.

Combine ingredients and serve at room temperature.

Enchilada Sauce

2   16 ounce cans whole tomatoes
2   teaspoons vegetable oil
1   medium onion, chopped
2   cloves garlic, crushed
3   tablespoons chili powder
½   teaspoons cumin
¼   teaspoons oregano
1   teaspoon salt

Sauté onion and garlic in oil. Add the remaining ingredients.
    Cover and simmer 30 minutes. If a smooth sauce is
    desired, cool and purée in the blender.

*Use this for for cheese or beef enchiladas. Makes enough for
24 enchiladas, approximately 4 cups of sauce.*

All Purpose Salsa

1½   cups fruit (tomato, avocado, peaches, mango, etc.) cut
        into small pieces, or 8 ounces of corn
¼   medium red onion, diced or 2 scallions, thinly sliced
½   red or yellow green pepper, seeded and diced
1   fresh or canned jalapeño, seeded and minced
1   tablespoon chopped fresh cilantro
2   tablespoons fresh lime juice
¼   teaspoon cumin

Simply combine the ingredients at least one hour be-
    fore serving time.

*Use for any combination of fruit (peaches, apples, nectarines,
grapes, oranges, etc.). For black bean and corn salsa, use ¾ cup of
each black beans and corn.*

Roasted Tomato Salsa

10   Roma tomatoes
1   large onion, quartered
2   poblano chiles, seeded
3–4 chipotle peppers in adobo sauce
2   cloves garlic, minced
        salt & pepper

Roast tomatoes, onion and poblano chiles in a 400° oven for
    25 minutes. Place in food processor with remaining in-
    gredients. Mince with on and off switch on processor.
    Easy to char vegetables in a skillet heated to medium high.

Tomatillo Salsa

1   *large onion, chopped*
2   *teaspoons oil*
2   *3½ ounce cans chopped green chiles*
2   *pounds fresh tomatillos or 4 10-*
     *ounce cans tomatillos**
2   *garlic cloves, finely minced*
1   *teaspoon sugar*
6   *fresh or pickled jalapeño peppers, seeded and chopped*

Sauté the onion in oil until transparent and limp. Do not brown. Add the remaining ingredients. Simmer about 25 minutes. Yields about 1 quart of sauce.

For tomatillo salsa verde, chill salsa and add fresh chopped cilantro.

About Tomatillos

*Tomatillos are small, sweet, green Mexican tomatoes. They are not unripe red tomatoes. Tomatillos are available canned and fresh. When fresh, they are covered with a pale green, papery husk. To prepare fresh tomatillos, remove husk by soaking tomatillos in cold water, rinse, and cover with water. Simmer 15 to 20 minutes. May be frozen in cooking liquid.

Mango Salsa

1   ripe mango, chopped
¼   cup fresh cilantro, chopped
¼   cup red onion, chopped
    juice of ½ lime
1-2 jalapeño peppers, chopped
    pinch of salt

Combine ingredients an hour or so ahead of time.
Cover well. Serve at room temperature.

Green Fanin Sauce
(Green Fah-Neen)

1   ripe avocado
1   green onion, chopped
1   cup Tomatillo Salsa
    juice of ½ lime
    water
    salt

Peel and slice the avocado. Place in blender or food
processor with onion, tomatillo salsa and lime
juice. Purée until smooth. Thin with a little water
until the consistency of gravy is reached.

*Delicious green dynamite! This sauce is served as a side dish
for Mexican Chicken, Salpicón, Green Enchiladas, Soft Tacos, and
green salad. Yields approximately 2 cups.*

Avocado Sauce

1	*avocado, cubed*
2	*tablespoons lemon juice*
1	*clove garlic, minced*
	salt & pepper
4	*tablespoons olive oil*
¼	*teaspoon salt*

Purée ingredients. Use for salad dressing or vegetable dip, also a great dip for flautas or taquitos.

Cilantro Salsa

1	*large bunch cilantro, chopped*
3	*green onions, minced*
1	*jalapeño pepper, minced*
1	*tablespoon lemon or lime juice*
1	*tablespoon red wine vinegar*
2	*tablespoons olive oil*
2	*tablespoons water*
	salt to taste

Combine ingredients and serve.
This can be made several hours before the event.

Mole Verde

4-5 *leaves romaine lettuce, chopped*
4 *cloves garlic, minced*
½ *cup fresh cilantro*
½ *pound or 2 cups quartered fresh tomatillos*
2 *large poblano chiles, seeded and quartered*
2 *cups chicken broth*
2 *tablespoons vegetable oil*
½ *cup roasted pumpkin seeds, lightly salted*
⅛ *teaspoon ground cloves*
⅛ *teaspoon ground allspice*
¼ *teaspoon cinnamon*

Remove husks from tomatillos (run under cold water) quarter and place in food processor. Add poblanos, garlic, lettuce and cilantro and ½ cup chicken broth. Blend until finely chopped. Pour into skillet and sauté over medium low heat in 2 tablespoons oil for about 25 minutes. Add more broth if needed. Meanwhile, grind pumpkin seeds until smooth and combine with ½ cup broth. Add to tomatillo mixture along with spices and cook 15 minutes more. Pour contents into blender and blend until smooth. Serves 4.

Use for an enchilada sauce or add cooked chicken and serve over rice.

Mole Roja

1   cup onion, chopped
3   cloves garlic, minced
½   cup slivered almonds
2   tablespoons vegetable oil
2   tomatoes, quartered
2   whole poblano chiles, roasted *
1   jalapeño pepper
2   tablespoons raisins
¼   teaspoon ground coriander
¼   teaspoon ground cinnamon
⅛   teaspoon ground clove
1   ounce unsweetened chocolate, chopped
2   cups chicken broth

Brown almonds in a heavy dry skillet until lightly
    brown and fragrant. Then add onions and gar-
    lic. Sauté in 2 tablespoons oil until the onion is
    translucent. Add chopped chocolate and stir un-
    til melted. Roast the tomatoes and chiles at 450°
    for about 25 minutes. Add to onion mixture
    along with the spices and chicken broth. Cook
    for about 25 minutes. Cool slightly and purée.
    Reheat before serving. Serves 4.

*Add cooked turkey and serve over rice, accompanied by black
beans. *Canned chiles can be substituted for the fresh.*

Rajas Poblano

6   poblano chiles
1   medium onion, sliced thin
3   garlic cloves, minced
3   tablespoons oil

Roast chiles for 15 minutes at 500°, turning until blistered and blackened. Place the chiles in a paper or plastic bag for 10 minutes to sweat. Remove skin, seeds and veins and cut into thin strips. Thinly slice the onion. Combine onion and garlic in heated oil. Sauté until translucent. Add chile strips and cook until heated through.

Two large tomatoes, peeled and chopped can be added after the chile strips and cooked for 5 minutes.

Pickled Fresh Jalapeño Peppers

20 *fresh jalapeño peppers*
1   *cup apple cider vinegar*
¼   *cup olive oil*
1   *teaspoon salt*
1   *teaspoon pickling spices*

Wash jalapeño peppers and pack tightly in pint jars. Combine remaining ingredients in a saucepan and bring to a boil. Pour over peppers leaving about 1 inch air space. Seal jars and process 10 minutes in hot water bath. Makes 2 pints.

Jalapeño Jelly

4-5 *fresh jalapeño peppers, ground*
1   *green green pepper, ground*
1   *cup apple cider vinegar*
5   *cups sugar*
6   *ounces of liquid fruit pectin*

Remove the stems and seeds from the peppers. Place in blender with water for easy blending, drain. Combine peppers, vinegar and sugar in a 3 quart saucepan. Bring to a boil and boil 4 minutes. Remove from heat and skim off foam. Add liquid pectin and stir. Makes five 6 ounce glasses. Pour into hot sterilized containers, seal with paraffin.

How To Cook a Chicken For Fillings

Boil 4 quarts of water. Rinse a 3 pound chicken well in cold water. Place the breast down in the boiling water. Add 2 teaspoons salt, 1 medium onion sliced, 2 ribs celery sliced with leaves, and 1 carrot. Return to a boil. Reduce the heat and simmer 20 minutes. Turn the chicken back side down and simmer 15 minutes more. Cool in the broth at least 30 minutes, then debone. A three (3) pound chicken yields 3½ cups of boned chopped chicken.

To cook chicken breasts, follow the same procedure but cook only 20 minutes (no need to turn) and allow to cool in broth and debone. Six breast halves yield about 3 cups.

Cut up the boned chicken with kitchen scissors and the meat will be more tender and less stringy!

Chicken, Tomato & Green Chiles

4	*cups cooked chicken*
1	*clove garlic, minced*
1	*medium onion, finely chopped*
2	*tomatoes, peeled and chopped*
1	*4 ounce can chopped green chiles*
½	*teaspoon salt*
¼	*teaspoon pepper*

Sauté onion in 2 tablespoons vegetable oil until soft. Add tomatoes, garlic and green chiles. Simmer 10 minutes. Add chicken and salt & pepper.

Use for burritos or soft tacos.

Seasoned Chicken

3   *cups chicken, cooked, boned, cubed*
1   *cup sour cream*
1   *tablespoon lime juice*
1   *jalapeño pepper, finely minced (more or less, as desired)*
2-3 *tablespoons green onion, finely minced*
1   *teaspoon cumin*

Mix together and marinate overnight.

Wonderful soft taco filling.

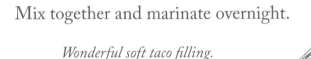

Spiced Ground Beef

1½ *pounds ground beef*
1½ *tablespoons chili powder*
1   *teaspoon cumin*
½   *teaspoon oregano*
¼   *teaspoon red pepper*
½   *teaspoon salt*

Brown beef in 1 tablespoon oil and add spices. Simmer over low heat 20 to 30 minutes. Add a little water if the mixture gets too dry.

Pork and Tomatillos

3   pounds pork, cubed
4   cloves garlic, minced
1   tablespoon oil
1   teaspoon salt
1   10 ounce can tomatillos
1½   teaspoons crushed red pepper
1   8 ounce can tomato sauce
½   cup water

Put cubed pork into pan, just cover with water, add
2 of the minced cloves of garlic and salt. Cover
and simmer 30 minutes. Drain and place in baking dish. Sprinkle with the oil and mix. Bake at
400° for 20 to 25 minutes. Meat should be crisp!
Blend the tomatillos and the crushed red pepper
together and then combine the meat, tomatillos
mixture, the can of tomato sauce, ½ cup water
and remaining garlic. Cover and simmer about
45 minutes.

Use as filling for burritos, chimchangas, tacos and taquitos.

Menus

Small Dinner Parties

Empanadas &
Guacamole
Fish Tacos
Green Enchiladas
Tamales
Lemon Sherbet atop
Baked Bananas

This would be a perfect menu for a patio party! Make grilled fish tacos. Everything can be made ahead except for the grilled fish. Everyone can gather around the grill while the enchiladas cook in the oven.

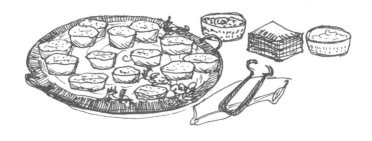

Mexican Chicken Portuguese is also perfect for very large parties. It is such a popular dish that guests always return for seconds or thirds, so be prepared! Make ahead and reheat in a double boiler or over very low heat, stirring often.

Nachos
Pico de Gallo (salad) with
Warm Flour Tortillas
Mexican Chicken
Portuguese
Tortilla Strips
Rice
Strawberry Sorbet &
Pralines

Dinner/Parties for a Group

Picadillo
Quesadillas
Chicken Chalupas
Beef Enchiladas
Chilaquiles
Pinto Beans
Chilled Fresh Fruits
Brownies &
Lemon Squares

Chicken or beef chalupas or fajitas with all the fixings make for a colorful table and also gives those who cannot cook a chance to bring something chopped!

This is truly a feast! When planning for the amount needed, allow one per person where applicable. Some will take half that amount and some more. It makes party planning a whole lot easier!

Summer Fiesta

Texas Cheesecake
Bowls of salsas with chips
Several kinds of Quesadil-
las, passed with Guacamole
Fish Tacos with condiments
Pica de Gallo (Salad)
Enchilada Suiza
Beans & Rice
Sliced Fresh Fruit Platter
Texas Chocolate Cake

Texas Cheesecake
Empanadas & Nachos
Hot Sauce with
Tostados
Gazpacho
Chiles Relleños
Chalupas
Green Enchiladas &
Chicken Enchiladas
Salpicón
Tamales
Pralines & Ice Cream

Sunday Night Supper

Quesadillas with
Guacamole
Salsa & Tostados
Chili
Rice
Pinto Beans
Fresh Tortillas with Butter
Guacamole on a Bed of
Chopped Lettuce
Sherbet or Fresh Fruit
Brownies

You might consider more
than one kind of chili with
condiments and beer!

Tostados & Salsa
Taco Salad
Enchiladas
Beans
Sorbet

Everything is a 'make ahead'.
Just reheat and enjoy the party!

Summertime Fiesta

Mexican Dip
Nachos & Empanadas
Chicken Fajitas
Cold Salpicón
Beans
Strawberry Sorbet

Luncheons

Find a beautiful, shady spot, dress up a picnic table with sunflowers, bright yellow napkins, a pitcher of Sangria and a few friends to enjoy the wonderful food.

White Gazpacho
Soft Tacos with Chicken
Mango Salad

Taquitos
Tortilla Soup
with condiments
Avocado & Grapefruit Salad

Chalupas
Fresh Fruit
Pralines

This has been the favorite luncheon for the tennis team, very easy to do with everyone bringing a dish, and, of course, this is the perfect luncheon for those who are dieting and those who are not.

Brunches

Huevos Rancheros
Tamales
Beef Enchiladas
Chilaquiles
Fresh Fruit Bowl
Brownies &
Lemon Squares

When entertaining a crowd, try to keep the menu to as many prepared ahead dishes as possible. If oven space is limited, heat ahead and cover with foil. Reheat just before serving.

White Sangria
Gazpacho
Eggs Mexicali
Cheese Garlic Grits
Black Beans
Tostados
Orange and Red Onion Salad
Pralines

Tequila Sunrise
Cheese & Green Chile Pie
Chilaquiles
Gorditas
Beans & Rice
Oranges & Red Wine

A Sunday brunch is a relatively easy party to give, especially since people tend to go home early.

Big Gatherings

Lots of Salsa,
Guacamole and
Tostados
Chili
Rice
Beans
Condiments
Jalapeño Cornbread
Pralines

Keep the menu simple and prepare lots! Surround with lots of condiments: sour cream, sliced jalapeños grated cheese, chopped onion. Make the jalapeño cornbread into muffins for easy reheating and serving.

Tex Mex Thanksgiving

Picadillo or Chili in Corn Cups
Fresh Chile Con Queso with Tostados
Raw Vegetables with Guacamole
Barbequed Turkey, stuffed with Tamales
Barbeque Sauce
Texican Squash
Mexican Rice
Borracho Beans
Flan

This feast is so good that you will wish for Thanksgiving more than once a year.

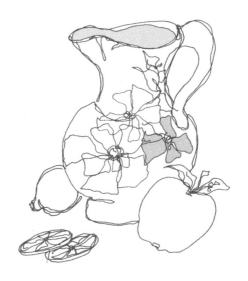

Drinks

Frozen Margaritas

1   *6 ounce can frozen limeade*
6   *ounces tequila*
3   *ounces Triple Sec or Grand Marnier*
     crushed ice to the top of the blender
     fresh lime
     kosher salt

Combine frozen limeade, tequila and Triple Sec or
Grand Marnier with crushed ice to the top of the
blender – blend until smooth. Prepare Margarita
glasses by rubbing the rims with a cut fresh lime
and then dip the glass rim into kosher salt. Spoon
in frozen Margarita. Serves 6.

*This is the basic recipe for Strawberry or Mango Margari-
tas. The basic recipe with additions can be made ahead. Freeze.
Twenty minutes before serving, remove from freezer. Garnish with
thinly sliced limes.*

Mango Margaritas

1   recipe Frozen Margaritas
2-3 fresh ripe mangoes

Peel mangoes and cut fruit away from the seed.
Blend fruit in blender until puréed. Combine
fruit with frozen Margaritas in blender or by
hand. Garnish with fresh lime slice. Serves 6.

Strawberry Margaritas

1   recipe Frozen Margaritas
1   pint fresh ripe strawberries

Clean and remove stems from strawberries. Place
strawberries in a blender and purée. Combine
with frozen Margaritas either in the blender or
stir together. Garnish with a slice of strawberry
and a slice of lime. Serves 6.

A short but important note about *Beer*. Plenty of ice cold beer is a must when entertaining with *Tex-Mex* food!

It is generally a good idea to have several varieties available, from light domestic beers, to heavily bodied, imported Mexican beers.

Margaritas (for 8)

8	*ounces tequila*
6	*ounces triple sec*
¾	*cup fresh lime juice*
	coarse or kosher salt
	lime slices to garnish
3	*ounces Simple Syrup (or more) see page 63*

Rub the rim of a cocktail glass with lime and then dip into a saucer of salt. Generously coat the rim. Combine the lime juice, triple sec, and tequila and pour into the glass with ice.

Margarita for One

1½ ounce tequila
½ ounce Cointreau or triple sec
2½ ounces lime juice, fresh
1 ounce Simple Syrup (see below) or more
salt and fresh lime

Combine ingredients in cocktail shaker with several
ice cubes and serve straight up or over ice.

Bartenders Simple Syrup

Bartenders Secret Ingredient!

Place in 1 pint jar – 1¾ cups sugar (fill sugar almost
to the top) – add boiling water to dissolve sugar.
Stir as you pour. Cover and cool. Keeps indefi-
nitely!

Orange Sangria

2   *cups freshly squeezed or reconstituted frozen orange juice*
1   *medium orange*
1   *bottle (⅘ qt.) dry red wine*
½   *cup Cointreau*
¼   *cup sugar*
    ice

Slice orange into thin slices. Combine 2 cups freshly squeezed orange juice (or 2 cups dairy orange juice), red wine, Cointreau and orange slices. Cover and chill. Serve in a bowl or pitcher.

Red Sangria

½   *gallon Burgundy or any dry red wine*
2   *apples, cored, sliced and unpeeled*
2   *lemons, juiced*
2   *oranges, juiced*
½   *cup sugar*
2   *ounces brandy (optional)*
1   *lime, sliced thin*
½   *gallon (2 quarts) soda water*

Combine the juice from the lemons and oranges with the sugar. Add the Burgundy and sliced fruit. (optional: brandy may be added to sliced fruit.) Just before serving, add the soda water.

White Sangria

½   gallon dry white wine
2   apples, cored, sliced and unpeeled or
2   fresh peaches, sliced
½   lemon, sliced thin
1   orange, quartered
1   lime, quartered
½   gallon (2 quarts) soda water
½   cup frozen lemonade concentrate *
½   cup sugar

Squeeze the orange and lime into a container and add
the sugar. Mix well. Add the wine and fruit. Just
before serving, add the soda water.

*Note: ½ cup frozen lemonade concentrate can be substituted
for the orange, lime and sugar. This is a refreshing summer-time
drink and it won't stain carpets or linens like red sangria.

Sangria Blanca

1	*bottle (750 mil) dry white wine*
½	*cup Cointreau*
¼	*cup brandy*
¼	*cup Bartender's Simple Syrup (see page 63)*
	lime wedges
	slices of lemon
	green apple wedges

Combine wine, Cointreau, brandy and Simple Syrup in a large pitcher. Blend well. Add soda just before serving. Garnish with fruit. Serves 6.

Tequila Sunrises

8   *cups of orange juice*
12 *ounces of tequila*
½   *cup grenadine syrup*

Combine ingredients. Serve over ice and garnish with orange slices. Makes 12 drinks.

Carefully layer the grenadine syrup on top by pouring down the side of the spoon. The effect is a sunrise!

Mexi Mary

6 *ounces Bloody Mary Mix*
2 *ounces tequila*
1 *whole green chile from a can*

Combine in blender. Serve over ice. Garnish with sliced lime and a celery stick. Serves 2.

For added heat, liberally add Tabasco® sauce.

Appetizers

Stuffed Jalapeño Chiles

Seed whole *Mild* jalapeños. Make a lengthwise slit to
remove seeds or simply cut in half lengthwise and
scoop out seeds. Stuff with grated cheese, tuna,
salmon or stiff guacamole. Use your leftover bits
and pieces! Chill and serve.

*These may be topped with a little sour cream and sprinkled
with paprika.*

Cheese and Green Chile Pie

1   *pound Monterey Jack cheese, grated*
1   *pound Longhorn cheese grated*
6   *eggs lightly beaten*
1   *15 ounce can evaporated milk*
2   *4 ounce cans chopped green chiles*

Combine the cheese, eggs and milk. Line a 9 by 13
inch Pyrex dish with the chiles and cover with
the mixture. Bake at 350° for 40 minutes. Cool
and cut into bite size squares and serve. Serves 12
to 15 people.

*A very popular appetizer and so easy to prepare. Cut into
larger pieces for a first course or use as a brunch dish - serving 6-8.
May be frozen and reheated.*

Chipotle Black Bean Dip

4 cups cooked black beans
1 large onion, chopped
2-3 cloves of garlic, pressed
3 tablespoons olive oil
2 (or more) chipotle chiles in adobo sauce*
1 tablespoon adobo sauce*
½ teaspoon salt
½ fresh lime, juiced
2 chicken bouillon cubes
½ cup grated Monterey Jack cheese
   fresh cilantro to garnish

Sauté onion in olive oil. Add garlic to mixture while still hot. Add beans, chiles and sauce, bouillon cubes, salt and lime juice. Cook at medium heat, mashing about ¾ of the beans, leaving some of the beans whole. Place dip in bowl while warm. Sprinkle with grated cheese and chopped cilantro. Serve with tortilla chips.

Chipotle chiles in adobo sauce are available in cans and always found in Latin American markets.

Jalapeño Olive Tomato Dip

1   10 ounce can tomatoes and green chiles
2   8 ounce packages of cream cheese
     - or -
1   8 ounce package cream cheese and 1 cup puréed
     cottage cheese
½   cup green olives with pimientos, chopped
¼   teaspoon Worcestershire sauce
½   teaspoon lemon juice
     salt & pepper to taste

Mix and chill, yields 4 cups of dip. Serve with tostados
   or raw vegetables.

Toasted Pumpkin Seeds

2   cups green pumpkin seeds (hulled)
1   tablespoon olive oil

Toast the pumpkin seeds in a cast-iron hot skillet,
   stirring until golden brown and puffed. Pour into
   bowl and add oil and salt.

     *Great topping for soups and stews, but unbeatable in a bowl
for snacking.*

Lone Star Bean Dip

2   15 ounce cans black eyed peas
1   10 ounce can tomatoes and green chiles
½   cup barbeque sauce
2   chicken bouillon cubes
2   cloves of garlic, minced
3–4 fresh jalapeño peppers, chopped
½   teaspoon cinnamon
¼   teaspoon nutmeg
1   teaspoon salt
1   medium onion, chopped
3   tablespoons oil or bacon drippings
    (add crumbled bacon if using bacon grease)
    several grounds of fresh pepper

Sauté onion and fresh chopped jalapeños and garlic
in oil or bacon grease until soft. Add remaining
ingredients. Bring to the boiling point. Reduce
heat and simmer 40 minutes or more. Mixture
will thicken to dipping consistency. Make a day
or two ahead. Flavor improves with age. Serve
with chips.

Green Chile Dip

2   *large tomatoes, chopped*
4   *green onions, chopped (stems too)*
1   *4 ounce can chopped green chiles, drained*
3   *tablespoons olive oil*
1½ *tablespoons red wine vinegar*
1   *teaspoon garlic salt*
     salt & pepper to taste

Combine the ingredients. Chill. Serve with tostados.

Jalapeño Bean Dip

3   *cups refried beans*
½   *pound Monterey Jack cheese*
1   *medium onion, chopped and sautéed in 1 tablespoon oil*
3-4 *medium jalapeños, finely chopped*

Combine all ingredients in a double boiler and stir
    until heated thoroughly. Serve in a chafing dish
    with tostados. Serves 12.

    *Scoop out squash shells or red/green peppers as containers for
dips and salsas.*

74

Fiesta Dip

2	avocados
1	tablespoon mayonnaise
2	tablespoons lemon juice
¼	teaspoon Tabasco® sauce
1½	cups Monterey Jack cheese, grated
1½	cups Longhorn cheese, grated
1	4 ounce can chopped black olives
1	medium onion, chopped
½	cup salsa
1	tomato, chopped
½	head lettuce, shredded

Combine avocados, mayonnaise, lemon juice and hot sauce; spread on a large dinner plate (or a shallow bowl similar in size). Next, layer in order the cheeses, olives, and onions. Combine the salsa and chopped tomato and add. Top with the shredded lettuce.

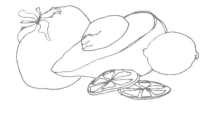

This dish can be made in the morning and served in the evening.

Black Bean Salsa

2 *cups black beans, cooked, rinsed and drained*
1 *tomato, chopped*
1 *small onion, chopped*
4 *scallions, chopped*
2 *cloves garlic, minced*
1 *or more jalapeño peppers, chopped*
2 *teaspoons cumin*
2 *tablespoons olive oil*
  juice of ½ lime
  salt & pepper
  fresh cilantro

Combine all ingredients except the cilantro and allow to sit for an hour or two, or make the night before. Sprinkle with cilantro and serve with tortilla chips.

Although homemade black beans are still the best, a quick substitute of the canned variety works well, too.

Monterey Jack Salsa

6   ounces pepper Monterey Jack Cheese, grated
1   large tomato chopped
3   green onions chopped
1   4 ounce can chopped green chiles
1   4 ounce can chopped ripe olives
½   cup chopped cilantro
    Italian Dressing (page 182)

Combine all of the ingredients. Add 1 to 3 tablespoons of Italian Dressing to help hold all together. Serve with tostados.

For a last minute get together, Monterey Jack Salsa is an
easy dish to assemble. Accompany it with a basket of multi colored
tortilla chips for a festive look.

Nachos

Basic Recipe:
Tostado chips
> *Grated Longhorn cheese or Monterey Jack*
> *Jalapeño slices*

Place the tostados on a cookie sheet (line with tin foil for easy clean up). Cover each tostado with a spoonful of grated cheese and top with a slice of jalapeño pepper. Broil until the cheese melts, 3 to 5 minutes. Watch closely. Nachos burn easily. Be creative! Nachos can be prepared a couple of hours before the event and then baked later. Place tortilla chips side by side. Select from the various options for toppings listed below. Bake at 350º for 8 to 10 minutes or until the cheese has melted.

Fillings:
*Refried pinto or black beans, grated
  cheese, jalapeño pepper slice
Leftover taco filling, beef or chicken,
  grated cheese, jalapeno slice
Grated cheese, slice of shrimp or
  chorizo sausage*

Always have a bowl of salsa accompanying the nachos for extra heat. Have bowls of sour cream, guacamole and/or avocado sauce for added toppings.

Quesadillas, Basic Recipe

6   *8-inch flour tortillas*
8   *ounces Monterey Jack cheese, grated*
1   *4 ounce can chopped green chiles*

Place the flour tortillas on a cookie sheet. Sprin-
     kle with cheese and top with one tablespoon
     chopped chiles or several slices of jalapeño pep-
     pers. Chopped onions and leftover taco filling
     can be added. Top with another flour tortilla.
     Bake at 400 º for 10 minutes. Cut into wedges
     and serve.
Quesadillas can also be made on a griddle. Lightly
     butter the tortilla and place buttered side down
     on a hot griddle. Top with cheese and chiles.
     Add another buttered tortilla on top. Lightly
     brown both sides. When the cheese melts, remove
     to a serving platter. Children love these - but easy
     on jalapeños for the kiddie batch. Serves 6.

Quesadillas, Variations

12 *8-inch flour tortillas*
    softened butter
½   *pound crabmeat*
1½ *cups sliced, cooked mushrooms*
3   *cups grated cheese*
1½ *cups shredded chicken*
½   *cup fresh cilantro*
1   *cup onion, chopped (raw or cooked)*
    sliced jalapeño peppers
1   *cup seasoned chicken (see Index)*
1½ *cups refried beans*
    whole shrimp, sliced

Lightly butter one side of the tortilla and place this side down on wax paper. Spread a thin layer of any combination of the fillings listed above, top with another buttered tortilla with the buttered side to the outside. If baking, bake at 350° 8 to 10 minutes. If using a hot skillet, place quesadillas on hot skillet for about 2 minutes then turn for another two minutes.

Quesadillas are always being reinvented with an increasing array of fillings and methods for cooking. They can be baked in an oven, browned in a hot skillet or placed on the outdoor grill. Whatever your choice, this is an easy colorful appetizer. Serve quesadillas with bowls of guacamole, sour cream, fresh tomato salsa or some of the fresh fruit salsas.

Chicken Quesadillas

2	cups chicken, cooked and finely chopped
1	jalapeño pepper, chopped
1	clove garlic, minced
½	onion, minced
1	tomato, peeled and chopped
¼	cup sour cream
	salt & pepper
	melted butter
12	8-inch flour tortillas

Sauté the onion and garlic in 1 tablespoon oil for 5 minutes. Combine with remaining ingredients. Spread 3 tablespoons of mixture on a lightly buttered tortilla, buttered side down. Top with another lightly buttered tortilla, buttered side up. Either bake at 350° 8 to 10 minutes or place on a hot skillet, turning when browned on one side or place on the outdoor grill. For crab quesadillas, simply substitute ½ pound of crabmeat for the chicken and proceed. ½ cup cheese can be added to either recipe.

Chili con Queso

1   *pound Velveeta® cheese*
1   *large onion, chopped*
1   *tablespoon vegetable oil*
1   *tablespoon flour*
1   *tablespoon chili powder*
1   *clove garlic (optional), minced*
1   *10 ounce can tomatoes and green chiles*
1   *chopped jalapeño pepper (optional)*

Sauté onion and garlic in oil until translucent. Add flour and chili powder. Cook 1 minute. Add tomatoes and green chiles and cook until sauce is thickened. Add cheese in chunks and cook until melted. Serve hot in a chafing dish with tostados. Yields 4 cups.

Add a cupful to cream of corn soup for a super lunch dish. Use as a sauce for leftover chicken. Make ahead, refrigerate to use as needed!

82

Fresh Chile con Queso

8   *fresh Anaheim or poblano chiles (or some of each)*
2   *cloves of garlic, minced*
1   *small onion, chopped*
2   *tablespoons oil*
1   *pound grated white Cheddar cheese*
2   *tablespoons sour cream*

Roast chiles over flame or place on a cookie sheet in a 500° oven for 10 minutes or until blackened. Place chiles in a sealed bag for about 15 minutes or until skin can be easily removed. Slice chiles, removing seeds and veins and chop. Sauté the onion and garlic in oil until translucent, about 10 minutes. Add chiles and cook about 10 minutes. Stirring constantly, add the grated cheese and continue stirring until the cheese melts. Add sour cream. Pour into a serving container and serve immediately with tortilla chips.

Texas Cheesecake

1½   cup tortilla chips, ground
4   tablespoons butter, melted
1½   pounds cream cheese, softened
4   eggs
1   4 ounce can chopped green chiles, drained
1   tablespoon cumin powder
1½   teaspoon garlic powder
2   teaspoons Mexican oregano
2   teaspoons chili powder
½   teaspoon salt
¼   teaspoon cayenne pepper
1   cup sour cream
½   cup chopped green onions

Grind tortilla chips in food processor. Add melted butter. Press mixture in bottom of 9 inch spring form pan. Bake at 350° for about 10 minutes. Beat cream cheese with an electric mixer. Add eggs one at a time and blend until smooth. Next, add spices and green chiles. Pour into prepared pan and bake 40 to 45 minutes or until set. Remove from oven. Cool and refrigerate. Can be made 2 or 3 days before the event. Serves 20.

To serve: Remove sides of pan and place on serving platter. Ice top with sour cream and sprinkle with green onion and cilantro or cover top instead with pica de gallo. Serve with plenty of tortilla chips.

Picadillo

1½ pounds lean ground beef
1   medium onion, chopped
2   tablespoons vegetable oil
1   teaspoon salt
1   clove garlic, crushed
1-2 teaspoons chili powder
1   8 ounce can tomato sauce
1   8 ounce can mushrooms, drained
1   16 ounce can tomatoes
2   tablespoons vinegar
1   teaspoon sugar
½   teaspoon ground cumin
1   teaspoon ground cinnamon
½   cup raisins
     pinch of ground cloves
½   cup sliced almonds

Cook the onions in oil until soft. Add ground beef and cook until browned. Add the rest of the ingredients except the almonds. Stir well and simmer covered for 1½ hours. Stir in almonds just before serving. Serve in a chafing dish (to keep warm) with tostados or Doritos®. This is best if made the day before serving. Yields about 2 quarts.

Picadillo stands alone as an appetizer or main dish served with rice. It is perfect as a filling for Empanadas or for Chiles Relleños (see Index). Serves 25 for dip.

Guacamole

4   *avocados*
1   *clove garlic, minced*
1   *jalapeño pepper, seeded and chopped*
2   *tablespoons lime juice*
⅓   *cup Pico de Gallo (see Index)*
1   *teaspoon salt*
½   *cup chopped cilantro*

Cube the avocado. Combine with remaining ingredients. Gently mash with a potato masher or fork. Don't overdo the mashing. This is best if chunkier. Serve with tortilla strips or jicama sticks.

Try substituting tomatillos for the Pico de Gallo. Simply remove husks and rinse 8 to 10 tomatillos. Broil until tender and slightly blackened. Mash. Add avocados along with remaining ingredients and mash. Leave some lumps.

Guacamole (for 6)

2   *ripe avocados, mashed*
2   *peeled tomatos, finely chopped (optional)*
2   *teaspoons grated onion*
2   *tablespoons fresh cilantro, finely chopped (optional)*
2   *tablespoons lemon juice*
     salt & pepper to taste
2   *dashes of Tabasco® sauce*

Combine all the ingredients and mix well. Return the avocado seeds to the mixture and cover tightly to prevent discoloration. Yields 1½ to 2 cups.

Serve Guacamole as a dip with chips, on a bed of lettuce garnished with tomatoes for a salad or on Chalupas.

Guacamole (for 30)

12 *ripe avocados, peeled*
1-2 *teaspoons ground coriander*
    salt & pepper to taste
    hot pepper sauce to taste
    juice of 4 limes
2 *ripe tomatoes, peeled and chopped*
1 *jalapeño, seeded and chopped*
1 *small onion, grated*

Mash avocados and add the remaining ingredients. Place several avocado seeds in the guacamole to prevent browning and cover tightly. Yields 6 cups.

Meat Balls in Chili con Queso

1½   pounds lean ground beef
1   package taco seasoning mix
1   medium onion, finely chopped
1½   cups crushed tostados
¼   cup Hot Sauce (see Index)
       Chili con Queso (see Index)

Mix the ground beef with taco seasoning mix, onions,
   crushed tostados and hot sauce. Form into cherry
   sized balls and brown. Add the cooked meat balls
   to hot Chili con Queso. Serve in a chafing dish.

Make ahead and freeze meat balls and Chili con Queso separately.
Serves 36.

Appetizer Corn Cups

6   *tablespoons butter, softened*
3   *ounces cream cheese, softened*
1   *cup flour*
½   *cup yellow cornmeal*
     pinch of salt

Combine the butter and cream cheese with a fork and
add the flour, ½ cup at a time until everything
is mixed. Add cornmeal and salt. Knead lightly
until smooth. Form into 1 inch balls and press
into small muffin tin rounds. Form small cups
with fingers, covering the bottom and sides of
molds. Bake 350° for 20 minutes. Yields 36 cups.

*Use any of the following for fillings (or make up something
new): picadillo, chili, seasoned chicken. Top with chopped lettuce,
sour cream or guacamole.*

Mexican Pie

2   cups refried pinto beans
3   avocados, mashed
2   tablespoons lemon juice
5   tablespoons diced onions, divided
⅛   teaspoon cayenne pepper
½   teaspoon salt
1   cup sour cream
½   cup mayonnaise
½   teaspoon garlic powder
1   teaspoon ground cumin
½   teaspoon hot pepper sauce
½   teaspoon chili powder
2   cups Longhorn cheese, grated
6   scallions, chopped
3   medium tomatoes, seeded & chopped
1   4 ounce can chopped black olives

Spread refried beans on the bottom of a 9" x 13" casserole. Combine the avocados, lemon juice, 2
tablespoons diced onions, cayenne pepper and
salt. Spread on the beans. Mix sour cream, mayonnaise, cumin, garlic powder, hot pepper sauce,
chili powder and 3 tablespoons diced onions.
Spread on the avocado mixture. Cover the sour
cream mixture with cheese, scallions, tomatoes
and black olives.

This can be made a day ahead.

Ceviche

1   *pound fresh bay or sea scallops or boneless white fish fillets, cut in small squares*
½   *cup fresh lime juice*
2   *jalapeño peppers, seeded and chopped*
2   *medium tomatoes, peeled and chopped*
1   *avocado, chopped*
6   *scallions, chopped*
4   *tablespoons fresh cilantro, chopped*
¼   *cup olive oil*
1   *tablespoon white wine vinegar*
    salt & pepper

The day before serving, wash scallops or fish, place in bowl and cover with lime juice. Tightly cover container and refrigerate overnight. The next day, remove scallops with slotted spoon and set aside. Stir the avocado in the lime juice, remove and add to the scallops. Reserve 1 or 2 tablespoons of lime juice. Add the remaining ingredients to the scallops and avocados. Season with salt & pepper and lime juice, if needed. Cover and chill till serving time. Serves six.

Empandas

Pastry for 60 empanadas:

1   *cup softened butter*
2   *3 ounce packages softened*
     cream cheese
2   *cups all purpose flour*

Cream butter and cheese. Blend in the flour. Form
    into a ball, wrap and chill overnight. Remove
    from the refrigerator 30 minutes prior to using.

 Roll out half of the dough ⅛ inch
    thick on a floured board. Cut out
    rounds with a large frozen juice
    can.

Fillings:

    Seasoned ground beef
    Picadillo
    Leftover chili
    Seasoned chicken

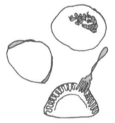

Place a rounded teaspoon on the dough. Fold, moist-
    en edge with water and seal with fork prongs.
    Bake at 400° for 12 to 15 minutes.

*Make these ahead and freeze. Place newly made, uncooked
empanadas on a cookie sheet. Put in the freezer until hardened and
then slip into plastic bags. Then add 3 to 5 minutes to cooking time.*

Tamale Appetizer

12   tamales, commercially prepared or homemade. See
      Tamales (Index) for directions.

Unwrap the steamed tamales, leaving them whole.
     Heat an iron skillet to 350º - 400º. Place tamales
     on the hot surface and turn as they brown. The
     results will be a crisp exterior. Cut these into bite
     size. Serve with guacamole.

> On a plane trip back to Washington from Texas, my
> seatmate shared this recipe with me when I told him that the large
> container on my lap, encroaching on his territory, contained tamales
> from Houston!

Jicama Sticks

Jicama (hee-cah-mah) is a root vegetable with a
     slightly sweet taste and a great crunch! Cut jica-
     ma into sticks. Sprinkle with fresh lime juice and
     dust with chile powder. Serve along with chips
     and guacamole.

Texas Caviar

1 16 ounce can black eyed peas, drained
1 16 ounce can white hominy, drained
2 tomatoes, chopped
½ cup, chopped onion
6 green onions, sliced
1 cup picante sauce
1-2 jalapeño peppers, seeded and chopped
2 cloves garlic, minced
¼ cup fresh cilantro, chopped
1 teaspoon cumin
1 teaspoon salt
1 teaspoon black pepper
1 teaspoon sugar

Combine all the ingredients and allow to sit several hours or more. Serves 12 for appetizers. Accompany with a basket of tostados.

Leftover Taco Fixings

Line cookie sheet, pie plate, or pizza pan with tostados. Sprinkle with meat mixture, chopped onions, chopped tomatoes, shredded Longhorn cheese and whatever else you like. Top with slices of Monterey Jack cheese. Bake at 400° until cheese bubbles, about 15 or 20 minutes.

Jalapeño Surprise

2	*12 ounce cans 'mild' jalapeños**
2	*egg yolks*
2	*egg whites*
½	*pound sharp cheese cut into fingers*
1	*inch hot oil*
½	*cup flour*
½	*cup corn meal*

Seed whole mild jalapeños (wearing gloves). Cut off stem end of jalapeños and scoop out seeds. Fill with cheese. Beat egg yolks until fluffy and pale yellow. Beat egg whites separately until stiff and fold into yolks. Stir flour and corn meal together. Dip stuffed jalapeños first into egg mixture, then into flour and corn meal mixture. Fry immediately in 1 inch of hot oil until crisp and golden brown. Drain and serve.

*These can be done ahead and reheated with a little sacrifice in crispness. *For the 'some like it hot' group – use the hot jalapeños.*

Green Chile Slices

1 cup Cheddar cheese, grated
½ cup flour
4 ounces butter, melted
¼ teaspoon salt
1 4 ounce can chopped green chiles

Mix cheese, flour and salt together. Add butter and knead until blended. Roll dough out thinly into a rectangular shape on a lightly floured board. Drain chiles and spread on dough. Roll dough like a jelly roll. Cover and chill. Slice and bake on a lightly greased cookie sheet. Bake at 350° for 10 to 12 minutes. Makes 2 dozen.

Add chopped jalapeños along with the chopped green chiles for added zip. Make ahead. Bake and freeze. Use as crackers for a soup course.

Rajas Poblano Appetizer

6   poblano chiles
1   medium onion, thinly sliced
3   cloves garlic, minced
3   tablespoons oil
1   cup beer
1   cup grated Monterey Jack cheese

Roast the chiles for 15 minutes at 500°, turning until blistered and blackened. Place the chiles in
a paper or plastic bag for 10 minutes to sweat,
then peel. Remove seeds and cut into thin strips.
Sauté the onion and garlic in oil for about 5
minutes. Add the chile strips along with the beer.
Cook at medium temperature until the beer has
been absorbed. Place chiles and onion mixture in
a flat ovenproof dish. Sprinkle with cheese and
place under the broiler until the cheese is melted.
Serve with tostados.

Soups
&
Chili

Black Bean Soup

1   *pound dried black beans*
1   *ham bone (or ¼ pound salt pork chopped into match sticks)*
2   *medium onions, chopped*
1   *carrot, chopped*
1   *stalk celery, chopped*
1–2 *cloves garlic, crushed*
½   *teaspoon salt*
1   *teaspoon pepper*
1   *bay leaf or laurel leaf*
¼   *cup wine vinegar, optional*

Wash the beans and pick out the rocks. Place the beans with all the ingredients (except vinegar) in 3 quarts water in heavy pot. Bring to a boil and simmer 1½ to 2 hours until the beans lose their shape. Purée. Add vinegar, if desired. Add more water or stock if too thick. Remove bones and bay leaf. Serve!

Top with a spoonful of sour cream and a dusting of chili powder. Or, serve garnished with sieved hard boiled egg, finely chopped green onions or a lemon slice.

Roasted Vegetable Gazpacho

2   pounds plum tomatoes, halved
1   onion, quartered
1   green pepper, quartered
1   tablespoon olive oil
3   cloves garlic, minced
2-3 tablespoons chopped, seeded jalapeños
2   cups V-8® juice or tomato juice
2   tablespoons red wine vinegar
1   cup water
2   teaspoons salt

Preheat oven to 500°. Place tomatoes, onions and green peppers in one layer. Lightly coat with olive oil. Roast 15 minutes. Turn vegetables and roast 10 minutes more. Cool until easily handled. Place contents of pan in food processor along with garlic, jalapeños and V-8® juice. Pulse on and off, leaving some chunks. Pour into a container and add the remaining ingredients. Chill several hours or serve hot with a dollop of sour cream mixed with a chipotle pepper in adobo sauce. Serves 8.

This is a great soup for anytime of the year but especially in the winter. Roasted vegetables take on a new flavor. Garnish with sliced green onions, homemade croutons or fried tortilla strips.

Summer Gazpacho

8	large tomatoes, peeled
1	large green pepper
2	large cucumbers, peeled
1	red onion
5	spring onions
4	large cloves garlic, pressed
2	tablespoons Accent®, optional
2	cups V-8® juice or tomato juice
1	quart water
⅓	cup vinegar
½	cup olive oil
1½	tablespoon salt
	freshly ground pepper to taste

Chop all the vegetables and combine with the rest of the ingredients. Save this recipe for those fresh, tasty summer vegetables. This will keep several days in the refrigerator. Wonderful for quantity making. Serves 12 to 16.

Green Gazpacho

3   *cucumbers*
2   *cups fresh peeled tomatillas or one 16 ounce can*
1   *green pepper*
1   *small onion chopped (or 4 spring onions with tops)*
2   *sprigs parsley*
1   *cup chicken broth*
1   *tablespoon vinegar*
      salt & pepper to taste
      hot sauce, if you wish

Blend or process all the ingredients. Chill well. Stir and serve with croutons. Serves 6 to 8.

Year 'Round Gazpacho

2   *one pound cans stewed tomatoes*
1   *teaspoon seasoned salt*
2-3   *mild jalapeño peppers, seeded and chopped*

Combine all the ingredients and blend in the blender or food processor until smooth. Serve well chilled with a choice of chopped cucumbers, green pepper, onions and tomatoes, crumbled bacon and croutons.

White Gazpacho

2   medium cucumbers
1   clove garlic, minced
1   pint sour cream
½   cup yogurt
1   cup chicken broth
1   tablespoon white vinegar
1   teaspoon salt
1   teaspoon white pepper
3   dashes Tabasco® sauce

Peel and dice cucumbers. Blend with garlic and chicken broth in processor. Mix sour cream and yogurt in a bowl. Add puréed cucumber mixture and season with vinegar, salt, pepper and Tabasco®. Chill the soup for at least 3 hours. (Overnight is best!) Serves 4.

Serve with chopped tomatoes, scallions, parsley, toasted slivered almonds and sunflower seeds – as garnishes.

Chilled Avocado Soup

4   *ripe avocados*
2½   *cups chicken broth*
      juice of 2 lemons
      salt to taste
1   *tablespoon chopped onion*
1   *cup milk*
2   *dashes Tabasco® or more to taste*
1-2 *tablespoons rum (optional)*
      toasted sesame seeds to garnish

Purée avocados, a little at a time, with some broth in a blender or food processor. Pour into a bowl and add the remaining ingredients. Seal tightly and chill 2 to 3 hours before serving. Serves 8.

Posole

1   *pound package dried homi-ny*
4   *jalapeño chiles, seeded and chopped*
2   *pounds fresh tomatillos*
5   *garlic cloves, minced*
1½ *cups chopped onion*
6   *cups chicken broth*
2   *cups water*
1½ *teaspoons salt*
4   *cups chicken, cooked and chopped*

Cook the dried hominy according to package directions. When done, about two hours, drain cooking liquid. Meanwhile, remove the husks from tomatillos and place tomatillos in pan with water to cover. Cook about 10 minutes and drain. Sauté chiles, onions and garlic in a small amount of oil until the onion is translucent. Combine the tomatillos and sautéed ingredients in a blender or food processor. Next combine hominy, chicken broth, water and puréed mixture in a large pot, and cover. Cook over medium to low heat about 30 to 40 minutes. Serves 10 to 12.

This is best made a day ahead and then reheated adding the chicken. Serve in bowls accompanied by an assortment of toppings: avocado, onion, radishes, lettuce, cilantro, all chopped, and lime wedges.

Pumpkin or Squash Soup

1   *large onion, chopped*
4   *cups cooked pumpkin or winter squash*
3   *cups chicken broth*
2   *cups milk or light cream*
     salt & pepper to taste
     Tabasco® or hot sauce to taste

Sauté the onion in a little butter. Put the pumpkin and onions through a sieve or food processor. Pour into a saucepan and add other ingredients. Heat, stirring, but do not boil. Serves 10.

Serve hot with a spoon of whipped cream or cold with a spoon of yogurt. Garnish with minced, tender spring onion and a sprinkle of chili powder. Do not prepare more than 24 hours ahead.

Summer Squash Soup

4   cups of summer squash, chopped
4   poblano chiles, roasted
1   onion, chopped
3-4 cloves garlic, minced
3   tablespoons olive oil
1   cup chicken broth or vegetable broth
1   cup buttermilk
    salt & pepper

Sauté the onion and garlic for 3 minutes. Add the squash and cover. Cook over medium heat 8 to 10 minutes, or until tender. Add the chiles. Transfer ingredients to a food processor or blender. Blend with the broth until smooth and add the buttermilk a little at a time for the desired consistency. Chill soup. Serve with a dollup of Lime Sour Cream.

Lime Sour Cream:

Combine and blend:
½   cup sour cream
2   teaspoons lime juice
½   teaspoon lime zest
1   teaspoon cumin.

Tortilla Soup

4   cups homemade chicken broth
4   ounces tomato sauce
1   medium onion, chopped
      salt & pepper to taste
4   tortillas
¼   cup vegetable oil
      chopped fresh cilantro to garnish (or parsley)

Cut the tortillas into strips and fry in oil until crisp.
In the same pan, cook the onions until limp. Add
the chicken broth and tomato sauce and bring to
a boil. Simmer 30 minutes. Place half the tortillas
in the soup. Use the remainder instead of crackers. Serves 4 to 6

Homemade Croutons

½ cup olive oil
2 cloves, garlic, peeled
3 slices bread

Soak the garlic in the oil for several hours, if possible.
Cut the crust off the bread. Slice the bread into
squares about the size of a dime. Heat the oil over
medium heat; add bread cubes. Sauté until golden
brown, turning frequently. Drain well. Sprinkle
lightly with salt. Makes 1½ cups.

*Once you have used these, you'll never use the store bought
kind again! For a change, try leftover cornbread, cubed and sautéed
in olive oil and garlic.*

Chuck Wagon Chili

2	pounds coarse ground beef (chili grind)
2	medium onions, chopped
2	cloves garlic, crushed
2	teaspoons cumin
6	tablespoons or more chili powder
1	teaspoon salt
2	16 ounce cans tomatoes
¼	teaspoon ground red pepper
1	tablespoon sugar

Sauté onions in vegetable oil. Add the garlic, meat and seasonings and brown. Add the tomatoes, cover and simmer 2 hours. Add the sugar during the last 30 minutes of cooking.

Prepare Chili at least a day before serving. A pot of good Chili needs time to mellow. Serves 8.

Vegetarian Chili

3   *tomatoes <u>or</u> 1 (one)14 ½ ounce can of tomatoes*
1½ *cups onions, chopped*
2   *poblano peppers, chopped*
3   *cloves garlic, finely minced*
3   *tablespoons olive oil*
4   *cups squash, diced — yellow and/or zucchini*
3   *fresh jalapeños, seeded and chopped*
4   *cups black beans, cooked and rinsed*
2   *cups pinto beans, cooked and rinsed*
4   *cups vegetable or chicken broth*
3   *teaspoons cumin*
2   *tablespoons chili powder*
     fresh cilantro

In a soup pot, sauté onions, garlic and poblano peppers in 3 tablespoons olive oil until tender. Add tomatoes, squash, jalapeños, cumin and chili powder. Cover and cook 8 minutes. Add remaining beans and broth and continue to simmer for 25 minutes. Serves 8.

Hen House Chili

1   pound Great Northern White beans, dried
6   cups chicken broth
2   cloves garlic, minced
2   medium onions, chopped and divided
1   tablespoon oil
2   4 ounce cans chopped green chile peppers
2   teaspoons ground cumin
½   teaspoon dried oregano
¼   teaspoon ground cloves
¼   teaspoon cayenne pepper
4   cups chicken, cooked and diced
3   cups grated Monterey Jack cheese

Combine beans, broth, garlic and half of the onions
in a large soup pot. Bring to a boil. Reduce
heat and simmer until beans are soft (3 hours or
more). Add more broth, if necessary. Sauté the
remaining onions in skillet until soft. Add chiles
and seasonings and mix well. Add to beans along
with the chicken. Simmer 1 hour. Serves 8 to
10.

*Serve with bowls of chopped tomatoes, scallions, and parsley,
chopped ripe olives, guacamole, sour cream, grated cheese and crushed
tortilla chips.*

Dynamite Chili

3   pounds chuck roast, hand chopped
1½   large onion, chopped
4   tablespoons vegetable oil
6   tablespoons chili powder
9   tablespoons flour
3   cloves of garlic, finely minced
1½   teaspoons salt
1   quart of water

Sauté the onion in oil until tender. Meanwhile, spread
   hand chopped beef on wax paper and work the
   chili powder, flour and garlic into the beef. Add
   beef to the onion mixture and cook 15 minutes,
   stirring constantly. Then add the salt and water
   and cook 45 minutes longer. Serves 6 to 8.

Serve with pickled or fresh jalapeños on the side for extra heat.

Pedernales River Chili

4   *pounds chili ground beef (see note page 117)*
1   *large onion, chopped*
2   *cloves garlic, minced*
1   *teaspoon ground oregano*
1   *teaspoon cumin*
2   *tablespoon chili powder (or more)*
2   *10 ounce cans tomatoes and green chiles*
1   *teaspoon salt*
2   *cups hot water*

Combine meat, onion and garlic in a heavy skillet. Sear until light colored. Add remaining ingredients. Bring to a boil. Cover, lower heat and simmer 1 hour. Serves 8.

When serving chili, the beans and rice (optional) should be served in separate bowls. A good pot of chili is not cooked with beans! To complete the presentation, have bowls of onion, jalapeños and cheese nearby.

Venison Chili

3   pounds venison, chopped or chili ground
2   pounds lean beef, chopped or chili ground
4   tablespoons bacon drippings (or vegetable oil)
3   large onions, chopped
2   16 ounce cans tomatoes
4   cups water
1   tablespoon salt
1   tablespoon pepper
5-6 tablespoons chili powder
1   clove garlic
3   tablespoons paprika
1   teaspoon oregano
1   teaspoon cumin
1½ teaspoons sugar

Brown meat in fat or drippings in a large heavy pan.
Add onions and garlic, cook until golden. Add
water and tomatoes; reduce heat and simmer
covered for about 3 hours, stirring occasionally.
Add the seasonings and simmer for another hour.
Serve immediately or cover and refrigerate or
freeze. Makes 1 gallon. Serves 8 to 10.

Ranch House Chili

3   *pounds beef, chili ground* *
2   *medium onions, chopped*
4-5 *cloves garlic, finely minced*
4   *tablespoons chili powder*
2   *teaspoons cumin*
1   *teaspoon salt*
2   *tablespoons vegetable oil*
3-4 *chipotle peppers in adobo sauce, seeded and chopped*
1   *12 ounce bottle beer*
1   *8 ounce can tomato sauce*

Sauté the onion and garlic in oil until tender. Add beef and stir until browned. Add seasonings along with beer and tomato sauce. Simmer, covered, for about 1 hour. Add water if mixture becomes too thick. Best made a day ahead. Serves 8.

*Chili ground beef is coarsley chopped beef. Ask the butcher or do it yourself. For a food processor, simply place 6 two-inch cubes of beef in the processing bowl and use a quick on and off motion to achieve a coarse ground. Meat can also be hand chopped.

Chile Verde

1   *pork tenderloin, cubed*
2   *tablespoons oil*
2   *garlic cloves, minced*
2   *10½ ounce cans chicken broth*
1   *onion, chopped*
4-5 *chile poblano, roasted*

Brown meat in oil. Remove. Sauté onion and garlic
 in same pan until soft. Return meat to pan and
 add other ingredients. Simmer 1½ hours.

Serve with pinto beans and rice. Leftovers perfect for bur-ritos. Serves 4 (or 8 to 10 burritos)

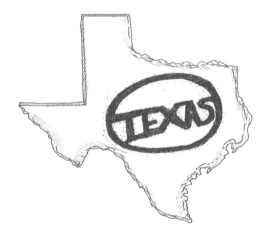

Long Horn Chili

3	pounds chili ground beef (see page 117)
3	medium onions, chopped
3	cloves garlic, minced
2	5 ounce can tomato sauce
2	12 ounce can beer
8	tablespoons chili powder
2	teaspoons cumin
½	teaspoon red pepper (or more)
1½	teaspoons salt

Sauté onions until soft. Add beef chunks and brown. Combine remaining ingredients. Simmer in a covered pan for 2 hours. Best made the day before serving!

For a hot and smokey flavor add 3 or 4 (or more) chipotle peppers in adobo sauce.

Salads

Molded Avocado Salad

2   *envelopes unflavored gelatin (2 tablespoons)*
¼   *cup cold water*
½   *cup boiling water*
5   *avocados (2 if using large Florida variety)*
2½ *to 3 cups fresh grapefruit sections (2 large grape-*
      fruit), chilled
½   *cup fresh lemon juice, chilled*
¼   *teaspoon salt*
1   *tablespoon sugar*
1   *cup fresh grapefruit juice, chilled*

Peel and purée 4 avocados, save one avocado to slice for garnish. Soften gelatin in cold water, add boiling water and stir until dissolved. Add the other ingredients which have been chilled. Pour into a 6 cup mold which has been rinsed with cool water. Chill until firm. Unmold and garnish with avocado slices.

Texas ruby red grapefruit slices and sliced avocado nicely arranged on a bed of mixed greens, lightly dressed with oil and vinegar or poppy seed dressing, is a great addition to any meal.

Taco Salad

1	pound lean ground beef
1	tablespoon chili powder
½	teaspoon ground cumin
1	clove garlic, pressed
½	teaspoon, oregano
¼	teaspoon dried red pepper
2	tomatoes, chopped
½	cup onion, chopped
1	cup grated sharp cheese
1½	heads, iceberg lettuce
1½	cups crushed Fritos®
2	avocados, peeled and sliced

Sauté the beef with the seasonings until done. Drain very well. Keep at room temperature. Combine and toss all the ingredients with the dressing. Dressing: Mix 2 tablespoons lemon juice and ½ cup of mayonnaise.

For individual luncheon servings, use crisp fried flour tortilla baskets. Vegetarians may substitute beans for meat.

A very easy luncheon dish... a nice change from Chef's Salad. Serves 8 to 12.

Taco Salad con Queso

1½ pounds lean ground beef
1   tablespoon chili powder
1   teaspoon salt
1   teaspoon cumin
1½ cups diced onion
1   cup celery, minced
3   cloves garlic, pressed
1   pound Velveeta® cheese
½–1 ten (10) ounce can tomatoes and green chiles
1   large head, iceberg lettuce
2   large tomatoes, chopped
1   6 ounce package Doritos® or tostados

Brown the meat with the chili powder, salt and cumin.
Sauté the onions, celery, green pepper, and garlic
until limp. In a saucepan, melt cheese, add tomatoes and green chiles and keep warm. Place the
chopped lettuce and tomatoes in a large bowl.
Add the meat and vegetables and toss. Then add
the broken Doritos® and pour the hot cheese
mixture over all. Serves 8 to 10.

Mango Salad

3   *3-ounce packages lemon Jello®*
1   *29 ounce can mangos, drained (save liquid)*
3   *cups boiling liquid (mango liquid plus water to make*
     3 cups)
1   *8 ounce package cream cheese*
     juice of 2 limes
     rind of 1 lime, grated

Dissolve Jello® in boiling liquid. Combine mangos and cream cheese in blender and blend until creamy. Add to Jello® and stir in lime juice. Pour into a greased mold and chill overnight. Unmold and serve on bed of shredded lettuce.

Mexican Jicama Salad

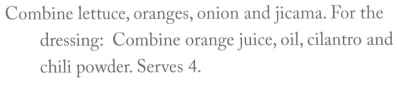

2   *cups torn lettuce*
2   *navel oranges, peeled and thinly sliced*
4   *thin slices red onion*
1   *cup peeled jicama sticks*
⅓   *cup orange juice*
½   *cup olive oil*
1   *tablespoon fresh cilantro, finely chopped*
¼   *teaspoon chili powder*

Combine lettuce, oranges, onion and jicama. For the dressing: Combine orange juice, oil, cilantro and chili powder. Serves 4.

Pico de Gallo (Rooster's Beak)

4	ripe avocados
2	tomatoes
1	medium onion
1	clove garlic, crushed
3	tablespoons lemon juice
1½	tablespoons juice from canned jalapenos
2	tablespoons olive oil
2	tablespoons fresh cilantro or 1 teaspoon dried
	salt & pepper to taste

Chop the avocados, tomatoes and onion. Add the remaining ingredients and mix well. Make this several hours prior to serving. Refrigerate covered. Serves 8.

Try spooning Pico de Gallo onto hot, buttered tortillas. Roll and eat! This wonderful dish was a featured selection in a restaurant in Matamoros, Mexico. Use Pico de Gallo as a condiment for fajitas. Note: Pico de Gallo is also included in the Basics chapter as a salsa.

Molded Gazpacho Salad

4   large ripe tomatoes, peeled
1   small cucumber
1   small onion
¼   green pepper
1-2   tablespoons vinegar
2   cups V-8® juice (or tomato juice)
      hot sauce or Tabasco® to taste
      salt to taste
¾   cup chicken broth, divided
2   envelopes unflavored gelatin (2 tablespoons)

Chop fine, blend or process the tomatoes, cucumber, green pepper and onion. Moisten the gelatin in ¼ cup broth. Then add ½ cup boiling broth. Next add the V-8® juice and the remaining ingredients. Pour into individual molds or one large ring mold. Refrigerate overnight or until firm. Serve on a bed of shredded lettuce. Garnish, as desired, with chopped cucumber, peppers, hard cooked eggs, parsley, scallions and avocado.

Molded gazpacho salad, black bean soup, and chicken quesadillas is a perfect luncheon menu. Add fresh fruit for dessert.

Egg Dishes

Huevos con Papas (eggs for two)

2   *small potatoes (size of lemons), chopped*
1   *tablespoon bacon drippings or oil*
2   *tablespoons chopped onion*
1   *tablespoon chopped green pepper*
1   *tomato, chopped*
4   *eggs, beaten*
½   *teaspoon ground coriander*
½   *teaspoon salt*
     Hot Sauce (salsa)

In a skillet, sauté potatoes in bacon drippings or oil until tender. Add chopped onion, pepper and tomato and sauté until tender. Stir in beaten eggs with salt and coriander. Cook and stir until eggs are set. Serve immediately with Hot Sauce and fresh flour tortillas

Easy one dish meal. Garnish with fresh parsley for an attractive luncheon dish.

Huevos Rancheros Migas

4   eggs, beaten
2   tablespoons bacon drippings
½   teaspoons Tabasco® sauce, or more to taste
2   tablespoons onion, finely chopped
2   tablespoons green pepper, finely chopped
¼   cup sharp cheese, grated
6-8 tostados, crumbled

Heat the bacon drippings. Add the eggs, Tabasco®
sauce, onions, and peppers. Cook over medium
heat. When the eggs are almost done, reduce the
heat and add the cheese and then the tostados.
Serves 2.

Migas means crumbs.

Skillet Huevos Rancheros

½   *small onion, chopped*
1   *tablespoon bacon drippings*
1   *tomato, peeled, if time permits, and chopped*
4   *eggs, beaten*
    salt & pepper
    Hot Sauce (salsa)

Sauté onion in bacon drippings until transparent. Add chopped tomato, cook for 2 minutes. Add beaten eggs and salt & pepper, stirring until set. Spoon on Hot Sauce, as much as you dare! Serve immediately with tostados and. Serves 2.

A great cold weather breakfast–one to get you rolling in any weather!

Huevos Rancheros

1   dozen eggs
1   teaspoon salt
2   cups Hot Sauce (salsa)

Pour the Hot Sauce (see Index) into a rectangular 2
quart pyrex dish and heat in the oven 10 minutes
at 325°. Break the eggs into a bowl and add salt
and stir. Pour into the pyrex dish on top of the
sauce. Sprinkle with chopped fresh parsley. Bake
at 325° for about 20 minutes or until eggs are set.
Serve immediately with crisp hot tostados. Serves
6 to 8.

*Great for hangovers served with Bloody Marys and an
extra bowl of hot sauce!*

Huevo Ranchero

1   fried egg
1   crisp fried tortilla
    Hot Sauce (salsa) to taste
    grated sharp cheese

Place a fried egg on top of the tortilla. Spoon on Hot
Sauce and top with grated cheese. Place under
the broiler until the cheese is melted. Serves one.

Gorditas with Chorizo

Gorditas are prepared from thick fresh tortillas, either homemade or store bought, but the thicker variety. There are two ways to prepare these little "envelopes."

Technique 1: Use a hot iron skillet, heated to medium high. Place fresh tortilla on the hot surface and gently tap with a spatula. The tortilla will begin to puff up. Remove and gently slit an opening on the side with a knife. Cover tortilla until ready to serve.

Technique 2: Heat about 1 inch of oil in a heavy skillet until medium high. Cut tortilla in half or leave whole. Place tortilla halves in oil and stir until they puff. Remove and drain. Slit the side of the tortilla with a knife to open it up.

Chorizo Filling:

1   pound chorizo sausage
1   medium boiling potato, cooked and diced
1   small onion, chopped

Remove sausage from casing and break into small pieces. Cook over medium heat until brown. Add the onion and cook until translucent. Add the diced potato and season with salt & pepper. To assemble, spoon filling into prepared gorditas and place on a serving platter. Serve with fresh salsa. These are a great addition to any brunch. Serves 10.

Eggs Mexicali

3 large tomatoes, peeled, seeded and chopped
1 medium onion, chopped
2 garlic cloves, pressed
3 tablespoons olive oil
4 tablespoons chopped green chiles
1½ teaspoons oregano
1½ teaspoons coriander
1 teaspoon salt
3 avocados
2 tablespoons grated onion
3 tablespoons lime or lemon juice
2 tablespoons olive oil
12 tortillas
6 poached eggs
1 cup grated Monterey Jack cheese

Sauce: Sauté the onions and garlic in the oil until limp. Add the tomatoes, chiles, oregano, coriander and salt. Simmer for 30 minutes. Mash the avocado and add the onion, lime or lemon juice and olive oil. Soften the tortillas in hot oil and drain on paper towel. Using approximately half of the avocado mixture, spread 6 of the tortillas with avocado. Place a tablespoon of the tomato sauce on each avocado spread tortilla. Place in a 9" by 13" casserole dish. Top with the remaining 6 tortillas and spread with the remaining avocado mixture. Place an egg on each top layer tortilla and top with the remaining tomato sauce and the grated Monterey Jack cheese. Bake at 450° for 4 to 5 minutes, until the cheese is melted. Serves 6.

This is a lovely dish for an elegant brunch, but for a hearty supper, use 2 poached eggs on each top layer tortilla.

Mexican Egg and Chorizo Casserole

3-4 *medium boiling potatoes*
3   *tablespoons olive oil, divided*
1   *medium onion, chopped*
2   *pounds chorizo sausage, removed from casing*
1   *16 ounce can of tomatoes*
2   *cloves of garlic, minced*
2   *tablespoons chili powder*
1   *teaspoon cumin*
8   *eggs*
1½   *cups light cream*
1   *teaspoon salt*
1   *teaspoon Tabasco® sauce*

Preheat the oven to 450° for the potato layer. Slice the potatoes in ½ to ¼ inch slices. Coat with about 1 tablespoon of oil, lightly sprinkle with salt. Layer across the bottom of a 9" by 13" casserole to form a crust. Sauté the onion in 2 tablespoons of oil until tender. Add chopped chorizo (remove from casing) and cook until lightly brown. Spread this mixture over the potato layer.

Prepare the tomato sauce by combining the canned tomatoes, garlic and spices in a saucepan. Cook about 20 minutes. Cool slightly and purée in a blender. Use about a cup of the sauce spread evenly over the sausage layer. Beat the eggs, add cream, salt and Tabasco®. Pour over the layers. Bake casserole at 325° for 40 minutes or until eggs are set. Serve with extra tomato sauce.

All of this recipe can be prepared a day or two before an event, except for the egg layer. Add that before baking.

Breakfast Burritos

Great for people on the run! Heat a flour tortilla either on a hot skillet, microwave or oven. Fill with scrambled eggs, scrambled cheese eggs, or any of the egg dishes in this section. Needless to say, great for leftovers. Wrap the fillings in the flour tortilla and then enclose the whole thing in foil.

138

Main Dishes

Chalupas Compuestas

Chalupas can be used as a salad, as a whole meal for
lunch, a light Sunday supper, or a buffet.
Begin with a crisp fried chalupa shell (warmed in a
250° oven for 5 minutes). Assemble with a layer
of each of the following:

Beef Chalupas:

Hot refried pinto beans
Seasoned ground beef
Grated Longhorn cheese
*Hot Sauce (salsa)
Chopped fresh tomatoes
Chopped onion
Shredded iceburg lettuce
Guacamole
*Hot Sauce (salsa)

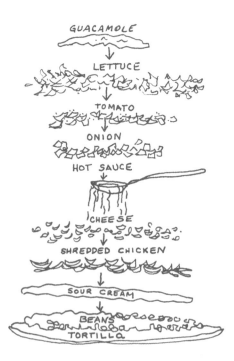

140

Chicken Chalupas

Hot refried black beans
Sour cream
Shredded chicken
Grated Monterey Jack cheese
*Hot Sauce (salsa)
Chopped onion
Chopped fresh tomato
Shredded lettuce
Guacamole
*Hot Sauce (salsa)

*There are differing opinions as to when the hot sauce
should be applied - let your taste be your guide
- some folks apply Hot Sauce at both points to
keep all the experts happy!

For a large party, served buffet style, chalupas are a grand
addition. The table will look very festive with either Mexican
bowls, or clear glass, filled with the colorful condiments.

Enchiladas

Just a quick note about Enchiladas. *All the enchilada recipes in this book are made with corn tortillas. For easier party preparation, make the enchiladas two or three days prior to the event, following these simple instructions.*

Spread a thin layer of sauce in the bottom of the casserole. Place the enchiladas side by side. Cover with foil. At this point they may be frozen. Thaw the day before the party. The day of the party, cover the enchiladas with sauce, sprinkle with cheese and bake.

When making enchiladas for a large party, put together an assembly line, softening 12 tortillas in oil, one at a time and stack on paper towels, blotting the oil as you go. Fill these. Repeat this process until you are finished.

Border Enchiladas (Beef)

3   *pounds boneless chuck roast*
½   *recipe Enchilada Sauce (see Index)*
½   *pound grated Monterey Jack cheese*
24 *tortillas*

Liberally sprinkle the chuck roast with garlic salt,
pepper and cumin. Bake in a covered pan at 275°
for about 4 hours or until meat easily falls apart.
When cool enough to handle, shred beef and
place in a bowl with one half of the enchilada
sauce. Marinate overnight. Soften the tortillas in
oil for enchiladas (see: Basic Techniques). Place
1½ to 2 tablespoons of meat mixture in each tortilla and roll. Place in a rectangular casserole, pour
the sauce over and top with grated cheese. Bake at
350° for 20 to 30 minutes.

*For an attractive touch, top with pepitas, toasted pumpkin
seeds.*

Rio Grande Enchiladas (Beef)

Sauce:

8   *tablespoons flour*
½   *cup vegetable oil*
2-3 *tablespoons chili powder*
4   *teaspoons cumin*
2   *teaspoon salt*
2   *cloves garlic, crushed*
5½ *cups hot water*

Brown the flour in a pan in a 500° oven (about 20 minutes. It will look like cocoa). Place the browned flour in a saucepan with the oil and add all the other ingredients except the water. Blend over low heat until smooth. Add the water slowly, stirring constantly. Simmer 2 to 3 hours, or until fairly thick. Cool and refrigerate overnight. Do not try to double this recipe.

Meat Filling:

1   *pound lean ground beef*
½   *teaspoon cumin*
1   *clove garlic, crushed*
½   *teaspoon salt*
2   *tablespoons hot taco sauce*
1   *tablespoon water, if needed*

Brown the meat. Add the other ingredients and simmer for 20 to 30 minutes. Add water, if necessary, to keep moist.

2	onions, chopped
1	pound grated sharp cheese
16	tortillas

Prepare the tortillas for enchiladas (see: Basic Techniques). Place the meat mixture, onions, and cheese on the tortilla, roll and place in a casserole. Heat the sauce and pour over the enchiladas. Top with cheese. Bake at 350° for 20 to 30 minutes.

Careful – don't overcook these! The sauce for these enchiladas takes time to make. It is very easy to make it several days ahead or weeks ahead and freeze.

Red River Enchiladas (Beef)

24   *tortillas*
1 ½ *pounds extra sharp Cheddar cheese, or Longhorn,*
      grated
2   *cups cooking oil*

Sauce:

1   *10 ounce can tomatoes and green chiles*
1   *16 ounce can tomatoes*
1   *clove garlic, crushed*
2   *tablespoons chili powder*
1   *teaspoon cumin seed*
4   *cups beef boullion*
      salt & pepper

Beef Filling:

2   *pounds lean ground beef*
1   *onion, chopped*
2   *tablespoons chili powder*
1   *tablespoon cumin seed*
      salt & pepper

Sauce: Put tomatoes, garlic, chili powder and cumin
    seed in the blender. Blend for 10 seconds in two
    batches, if necessary. Pour into saucepan and add
    beef boullion and simmer for 20 minutes. Correct
    seasoning.

Beef Filling: Sauté onions in a little oil until golden.
    Add the meat and brown. Drain off the fat and

add salt, pepper, chili powder, cumin and 1 cup of sauce. Soften the tortillas in oil and then dip in the sauce. Fill with about 2 tablespoons meat and 2 tablespoons cheese and roll. Place one layer side by side in 2 shallow rectangular casseroles. Sprinkle generously with grated cheese. (This much may be completed ahead or even frozen if desired. Freeze the sauce separately.)

Pour the remaining sauce over each casserole just before cooking. Cover very loosely with foil and heat at 325° for 20 to 30 minutes. Do not overcook.

Green Chicken Enchiladas

8	*chicken breast halves*
1	*onion*
3	*cloves garlic, peeled, divided*
4	*10 ounce cans tomatillas*
4	*green onions*
2	*jalapeño peppers*
1	*bunch parsley*
2	*cups chicken broth (from cooking of chicken breasts)*
½	*teaspoon cumin*
½	*teaspoon pepper*
	salt to taste
2	*tablespoons vegetable oil*
¾	*pound Monterey Jack cheese, grated*
1	*small onion, chopped*
16	*tortillas*

Stew the chicken breasts in water to cover, with onion, 1 clove of the garlic, salt & pepper. Cool and
shred. Reserve broth. Place shredded chicken,
grated cheese and chopped onion in bowl. Toss
with fork to combine.

Sauce: In a blender, place tomatillas, green onions,
jalapeños, parsley, 2 cloves of the garlic, 2 cups
of chicken broth, cumin and pepper. Blend until smooth. Place the oil in a skillet and add the
sauce and ½ teaspoon salt. Reduce by one fourth.

Soften tortillas in oil for enchiladas. Fill each tortilla with 2 heaping tablespoons onion, shredded cheese and chicken mixture. Arrange in a single layer side by side in a 9" by 13"casserole. Cover with the sauce. Bake at 325° for 20 to 30 minutes. Serves 8.

Chicken Enchiladas

2   chickens (4 to 5 lbs. each)
2   ribs celery, cut in pieces
2   carrots, cut in pieces
2   garlic cloves, peeled
        salt & pepper
1-2   tablespoons ground cumin
2   green peppers, chopped
2   medium onions, chopped
3   tablespoons vegetable oil
1   4 ounce can green chiles, chopped
2   teaspoons chili powder
1   teaspoons garlic powder
1   pound sharp Cheddar cheese, grated
32   tortillas
2   cups chicken broth
1   5 ounce can evaporated milk
1   10 ¾ can condensed cream of chicken soup
1   10 ounce can tomatoes and green chiles
½   pound Monterey Jack cheese,
        grated

Make a broth with the celery,
    carrots, garlic, salt & pep-
    per and water to just cover.
    Add the chickens and poach them until tender,
    about 1½ hours. Remove chickens from broth.
    When cool, remove meat from bones and shred
    it. Stir cumin into broth and put it aside.

Sauté the green peppers and onions in oil. Scrape into a bowl and mix in green chiles. Combine chili and garlic powders and put into an empty spice bottle or another container with a shaker top.

Use two 9" x 13" pyrex casserole dishes. Pour ½ cup broth in bottom of each casserole. Dip a tortilla in hot chicken broth briefly to soften it. Then spread with small amounts of chicken, peppers and onion mixture, grated cheese, and a generous shake of the chili and garlic powder seasoning. Roll up the tortillas placing each enchilada in the casserole as it is rolled, making a single layer. Pour 2 cups of broth with the evaporated milk and condensed soup into a saucepan. Stir together and heat to make a sauce. Pour it over the enchiladas. Add the tomatoes (undrained) and place the casserole in a preheated 325° oven. Cook for 45 minutes. Add Monterey Jack for final 10 minutes. Serves 18.

The tortillas in this recipe can be softened in hot oil instead of hot chicken broth.

Lone Star Enchiladas (Chicken)

3   *cups cooked, diced chicken (see* How to Cook a Chicken*)*

1   *10 ounce can tomatoes and green chiles*

1   *16 ounce can of tomatoes*

1   *clove garlic, crushed*

1   *large onion, chopped*

¾   *teaspoon coriander*

1   *teaspoon salt*

2   *cups sour cream*

1   *pound sharp cheese, grated*

16   *tortillas*

Combine tomatoes, garlic, onion, coriander and salt in a blender. Pour into a pan and simmer 30 minutes. Remove from heat, cool slightly and stir in sour cream. Soften tortillas in hot oil and then dip in sauce. Spoon chicken and cheese into each tortilla, roll and put in a casserole dish side by side. Just before cooking, pour remaining sauce over enchiladas and sprinkle with cheese. Bake at 325° for 30 minutes. Serves 8.

Green Enchiladas (Spinach)

24   tortillas
4   medium onions, chopped
1½   pounds Monterey Jack cheese, grated
2   10¾ ounce cans cream of chicken soup
1   10 ounce package frozen, chopped spinach, thawed
      and drained
¼   cup minced green onions
2-3   jalapeño peppers, seeded and chopped
¼   teaspoon salt
2   cups sour cream

Combine spinach, green onions, soup and jalapeños
    in blender and blend until smooth. Add the sour
    cream. Set aside. Prepare the tortillas for enchila-
    das by softening in hot oil. Fill the tortillas with
    approximately 1 tablespoon onion and 1 heaping
    tablespoon or more of cheese, and roll. Place in a
    9" by 13" casserole and cover with the green spin-
    ach sauce. Sprinkle with the remaining cheese.
    Bake at 325° for 30 minutes. Serves 12.

*The most requested enchilada
dish north of the border. Even people
who think they don't like spinach, love
these.*

Enchiladas Suizas

1   medium onion, chopped
2   tablespoons vegetable oil
1   clove garlic, minced
2   cups tomato sauce
2   4 ounce cans chopped green chiles
3   cups chicken, cooked and chopped
16 tortillas
6   chicken bouillon cubes
3   cups half and half cream
½   pound Monterey Jack cheese, grated

Sauté onion in oil until soft. Add garlic, tomato sauce, green chiles and chicken. Simmer for 10 minutes and add salt if needed. Soften the tortillas in oil for enchiladas (see Basics). Dissolve bouillon cubes in hot cream. Dip softened tortillas in the cream mixture. Fill with the seasoned chicken. Roll and place seam side down in a 9" x 13" casserole. Pour the remaining cream over the enchiladas and cover with cheese. Bake at 350° for 30 minutes. Serves 8.

Cheese Enchiladas

24   *tortillas*
2   *medium onions, chopped*
1½   *pounds cheese, grated (Longhorn or Monterey Jack, or*
     a combination)
1   *recipe Enchilada Sauce (see Index)*

Soften tortillas in hot oil for enchiladas. Fill each tortilla with a generous heaping tablespoon cheese
and a half tablespoon of onion. Roll. Place in a 9"
by 13" casserole. Pour the sauce over just before
baking and top with the remaining cheese. Bake
at 350° for 20 to 30 minutes. Serves 8.

Cheese Enchiladas topped with "leftover" chili and grated
cheese are delicious!

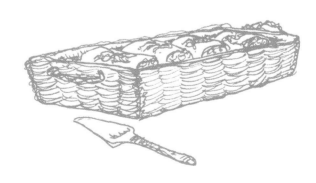

Mexican Crépas

½   cup yellow corn meal
½   cup boiling water
3   eggs, beaten
½   teaspoon salt
½   cup sifted all-purpose flour
1   tablespoon butter, melted
¾   cup milk
1   large onion, chopped
1   tablespoon vegetable oil
3   cloves garlic, crushed
3   small serrano chiles, chopped
2   8 ounce cans tomato sauce
    salt & pepper to taste
¾   pound lean ground beef, cooked
1½ cups sour cream
1½ cups chopped and lightly mashed avocado
½   pound sharp Cheddar cheese, grated

Combine corn meal and boiling water, stir well and
let cool. Add eggs, salt, flour and melted butter.
Mix until smooth, and then stir in milk. Heat a 6
inch skillet to medium high. Lightly brush with
melted butter. Pour in 1 tablespoon batter. When
the crepe begins to bubble, turn over and quickly
cook the other side. Makes 12 crepes. Set aside.
Sauté onion in oil until softened. Add garlic,
serrano chiles, and tomato sauce and chili pow-

der. Cook over low heat for an hour. Taste and season with salt, pepper and more chili powder, if desired.Divide this sauce equally between two bowls and stir the beef into one of them. Line each crepe with equal amounts of meat sauce, sour cream and guacamole and roll up. Place in a single layer in a casserole or baking dish and cover with meatless sauce and shredded cheese. Place in a preheated 325° oven until heated through, about 30 minutes. Serves 6.

Smoked Turkey
Stuffed with Tamales

1   15 pound turkey
    Barbeque Sauce (see below)
3   dozen tamales

Smoke the turkey in a covered heavy-duty smoker
    grill. Baste frequently with the sauce. Cook over
    low heat for 8 to 10 hours. Use charcoal with
    hickory or mesquite chips. Test for doneness
    as you would an oven-baked turkey. When the
    turkey is done, stuff with the warm, shucked and
    broken tamales. Baked at 250° for 30 minutes.
    Use the barbeque sauce for gravy.

*Crumbled, re-cooked tamales are a delightfully different
dressing – not unlike cornbread stuffing – a delicious surprise for a
buffet supper!*

Barbeque Sauce

1   cup ketchup
2   cups vinegar
½   cup vegetable oil
½   cup butter, melted
3   tablespoons sugar
1   large onion, grated
4   cloves garlic, minced
¼   cup Worcestershire sauce
1   lemon, juiced

2   tablespoons dry mustard
3   tablespoons chili powder
2   teaspoons salt
2   teaspoons pepper

Combine ingredients and simmer 20 minutes.

Cabrito Asada (baby goat)

Cabrito is a popular meat for barbeques in south Texas
and Mexico. Have the butcher split and clean the
whole baby goat. Marinate the meat in the coffee
mop sauce (see page 171) for 4 hours. Grill very
slowly over a low fire until tender, turning and
mopping frequently.

Chiles Relleños

(Choice of Picante or Spicy Raisin and Olive Filling)

Picante Filling:

1½   pounds ground beef
1½   teaspoons chili powder
1   teaspoon cumin
½   teaspoon oregano
¼   teaspoon red pepper
1   8 ounce can tomato sauce
1   medium onion, chopped
2   cloves garlic, minced
½   pound Monterey Jack cheese, grated
     salt & pepper to taste
1-2 jalapeño peppers, seeded and chopped

Sauté the onion and garlic in 2 tablespoons oil. Add
the beef and brown. Combine the remaining ingredients except cheese. Simmer 30 minutes, then
add the cheese, stirring until melted.

Spicy Raisin and Olive Filling:

1½   pounds ground beef
1   medium onion, chopped
2   cloves garlic, minced
1   tablespoon parsley
1   cup pecans or walnuts, broken
1   cup raisins

Sauté the onion and garlic in 2 tablespoons oil. Add
the beef and brown. Combine the remaining
ingredients. Simmer 30 minutes.

3 cans whole green chiles or 12 chiles poblanos (fresh)

If you are using canned chiles, rinse, remove any seeds,
and pat dry. For fresh chiles poblanos, roast for
15 minutes at 500° turning until blistered and
blackened. The chiles can also be roasted over a
gas flame using a long fork. Either way, place the
chiles in a paper or plastic bag for 10 minutes
to sweat and then peel. Carefully place about
2 tablespoons of filling in the chiles and gently
reform.

Beer Batter:
1½ cups beer
1½ cups flour

Add beer to flour and wisk until smooth. Allow batter
to rest covered and unrefrigerated for at least 3
hours. Roll stuffed chiles in flour, dip in beer batter and fry immediately in vegetable oil heated
to 350°. Use about 1 inch oil in a skillet or deep
fat fry. Fry until golden brown on both sides and
drain on a wire rack over a large brown bag with
a cookie sheet under everything. These are best

served right away or if you must, place the chiles on a wire rack and cookie sheet in a 200° oven for a short time. Serves 12.

Chili Relleños in Casserole

4   *ounces Monterey Jack cheese, strips*
1   *cup grated sharp cheese*
1   *4 ounce can whole green chiles, seeded*
4   *eggs*
½   *cup milk*
½   *cup flour*
½   *teaspoon baking powder*

Stuff chiles with Monterey Jack cheese strips and place in a lightly greased casserole dish. Beat eggs until thick and add other ingredients. Pour over chiles. Sprinkle with grated sharp cheese. Bake at 375° for 30 minutes. Serves 4.

Chorizo (Mexican Sausage)

1	pound ground lean pork
1	teaspoon salt
2	tablespoons chili powder
¼	teaspoon cumin
½	teaspoon oregano
2	cloves garlic, pressed
2	teaspoons vinegar

Mix all ingredients. Form into patties and fry without oil. This is best if allowed to sit overnight in the refrigerator and then made into patties.

Serve for breakfast or brunch with Huevos Rancheros. Form into meatballs and serve with Hot Sauce (salsa) for an interesting appetizer. Better yet, use instead of seasoned beef in Chalupas Compuestas.

Mexican Chicken

1   *tablespoon butter*
1½ *teaspoons ground cumin*
1   *teaspoon salt*
½   *teaspoon chili powder*
1   *3 pound chicken*

Rub the chicken with 1 tablespoon butter. Place ½ medium onion, sliced; a rib of celery with leaves, cut in sticks; a carrot; and a few sprigs of parsley in the body cavity. Tie the legs together and sprinkle the chicken liberally with the combined spices. Place in a shallow pan in a 450° oven. After 10 minutes, reduce the heat to 325° and bake for 45 minutes or until done (the leg bone moves easily). Serve with Mexican rice and an avocado and grapefruit salad for an easy, low calorie supper.

Chicken breasts may also be cooked with these spices on a bed of the vegetables with a delicious result – reduce cooking time to 30 minutes.

Mexican Chicken Portuguese

6	cups cooked, chopped chicken
1	pound Velveeta® cheese, cut in chunks
1	pound Longhorn cheese, grated
1	pint sour cream
1	3 ounce jar sliced pimientos
2	10 ounce cans tomatoes and green chiles
3	medium onions, chopped
1	clove garlic, minced
1	tablespoon oil
2	green peppers, seeded and chopped (optional)

Cook the onion and garlic in oil until transparent. Add the tomatoes and green chiles and bring to a boil. Reduce the heat and simmer until thick, about 20 minutes. Add the cheeses and heat slowly until melted. Then add the chicken and sour cream. Heat until hot and smooth, but do not boil. Serve over a layer of rice and a layer of crisp tostado strips. Serves 12.

Easy to make and a real party pleaser! Be generous when planning for a crowd, as everyone always goes back for seconds and even thirds.

Tamales

Recipe makes 24.
First prepare corn husks by soaking in warm water 3 to 4 hours or
overnight.

Filling:

3   *full cups cooked, lean pork roast (save some of the fat*
      trimmings)
1   *10 ounce can tomatoes and green chiles*
1   *medium onion, chopped*
1-2 *cloves garlic, pressed*
1   *tablespoon chili powder*
1   *teaspoon salt*

Combine the tomatoes and green chiles, onion, garlic,
chili powder and salt in a saucepan and simmer
30 minutes until thickened. Shred the pork (a
food processor is ideal for this). Mix the sauce
and meat together and set aside. Chicken, turkey
or beef may be used instead of pork.

Dough:

3   *cups masa*
1½   *cups shortening (use the fat trimmings from the pork for*
      added flavor)
½   *cup chicken broth*

Place the masa, shortening and pork trimmings in
the food processor and gradually add the chicken

broth. Process until mixture is very fluffy (masa will float on top when dropped into a cup of cold water). More broth can be added, a tablespoon at a time if masa seems too thick to spread easily.

To Assemble:

Spread husks with masa, placing 1 heaping tablespoon masa in middle of husk and spreading as shown. Spread 1 heaping tablespoon filling, as shown. Roll, beginning with filled edge, and fold up bottom of husk. Place on flat surface with fold underneath.

Steaming:

Steam cook tamales by placing them upright on folded end in steamer. To improvise a steamer, invert a pie tin, punched with holes as a support for another foil pie tin (punch numerous small holes to let the steam circulate) and place in a large kettle. Pour about 1 inch of water in the kettle; cover tightly and steam 2 hours.

Check water level frequently. Tamales are done when one can be unrolled, clear and free of the husk.

Don't eat the corn husk!

Venison Tamales

Venison is usually very lean, but is delicious as a tamale filling when mixed with an equal amount of pork. Use 1½ cups of cooked venison (leftover from a roast) and 1½ cups of pork to make 3 cups of meat for the tamale filling and proceed with the tamale recipe.

Duck Tamales

Hunters in your family? Or have you leftover Long Island duckling? Use 3 cups cooked and shredded duck in place of the pork for the filling.

Be careful to remove all bones!

Tacos

The best known Mexican dish - The Mexican Sandwich. Begin with a crisp fried taco shell (warmed
in a 250° oven for 5 minutes). Then fill with:

Spiced Ground Beef (see Index) or shredded chicken

Grated Longhorn cheese

Chopped fresh tomatoes

Shredded iceberg lettuce

Chopped onion

Hot Sauce (salsa)

For vegetarians, substitute refried beans or rajas poblano.

Crowd Pleasing Soft Tacos

12   *corn tortillas, or more*
3   *cups filling: beef, chicken, or pork*
1   *cup vegetable oil*

Heat oil in heavy skillet to 350°. Quickly dip the tortilla in oil to soften and pat off excess oil. Fill the tortilla with 2 to 3 tablespoons filling and fold. Place the folded tacos on a wire rack ,which fits over a cookie sheet. Bake at 400° for 10 to 12 minutes. Have bowls of condiments ready.

For appetizers, use 4-inch corn tortillas and proceed. Special order tortillas come from suppliers and tortilla factories. Some detective work is needed but they can be located.

Serve with bowls of chopped tomatoes, jalapeños, lettuce, onion, grated cheese and lots of salsa.

Carne Asada   *Tex Mex Grilling*

1   *flank steak*

Coffee Mop Sauce:

½   *cup tomato sauce*
1   *cup strong black coffee*
¼   *cup Worcestershire sauce*
1   *tablespoon sugar*
1   *teaspoon salt*
1   *tablespoon pepper*
1   *stick (8 ounces) butter*

Combine and simmer 20 minutes and cool. Marinate
the flank steak in the coffee mop sauce several
hours. Grill over charcoal, generously mopping
frequently. The mop sauce is also good for mari-
nating and basting grilled beef, chicken, pork,
lamb and venison.

Burritos

Chicken, Pork, Bean, Beef, Vegetarian

Whole books have been written on burritos. However, one quick paragraph should be enough to educate the novice. Begin with flour tortillas. Tightly wrap the tortillas in foil. Heat in a 350°oven for 15 minutes. For 8-inch flour tortillas, place 3 tablespoons of heated filling in the center of the tortilla and fold the right and left sides of the tortilla to partially cover the filling. Roll the tortilla from bottom to top to fully enclose the filling. Serve immediately.

Suggested fillings:

Chicken, tomato and green chiles
Leftover roasted chicken
Carnitas
Pork and tomatillos
Chili
Black beans
Pinto beans
Rajas poblano

Welcome additions: Chopped onion, tomato, lettuce, cheese, guacamole and sour cream. Note: For heartier appetites use the 12-inch flour tortilla and load up!

172

Beef Burritos

1   *recipe Chiles Verdes con Carne (see Index)*
1   *medium onion, minced*
2   *cups Monterey Jack or Longhorn cheese, grated*
12 *8-inch flour tortillas*

Tightly wrap the tortillas in foil. Heat in 350° oven for
15 minutes. Using a slotted spoon, place the meat
filling in the tortilla. Sprinkle with onion and
cheese. Fold the right and left sides of the tortilla
to partially cover the filling. Roll the tortilla from
bottom to top, and serve immediately. These are
quick, and everyone can make their own if you
like. Serves 12.

Bean Burritos

Follow the same procedure as in Beef Burritos for
heating the tortillas. Spread each tortilla with 3
tablespoons hot refried beans (see Index). Top
with some or all of the following toppings: grated
cheese, chopped onions, shredded lettuce, sour
cream, guacamole, salsa. Fold the right and left
sides of the tortilla to partially cover the filling.
Roll the tortilla from bottom to top.

Chimichangas

2½ pounds stew beef
3 cloves garlic, minced
1½ teaspoons cumin
3 tablespoons chili powder
1 onion, sliced
1 teaspoon salt
½ teaspoon pepper
6 8-inch flour tortillas

Place cut up stew beef and seasonings in a sauce pan. Add enough water to cover beef. Simmer covered about 2 hours or until meat is tender. Reserve broth. Shred beef when cool enough to handle. Moisten shredded beef with ½ cup of cooking broth. Add more salt & pepper, if needed. Wrap the tortillas tightly in foil. Bake at 350° for 15 minutes. Place 3 to 4 tablespoons of beef in the tortillas . Fold the right and left sides of the tortilla to partially cover the filling. Roll the tortilla from bottom to top. Heat about 1 inch of oil in a skillet to 350°. Place the rolled tortillas seam side down in the skillet. Fry 2 or 3 at a time, 1 minute per side, or until golden. Serve on a bed of chopped lettuce. Top with sour cream and guacamole and pass the salsa. Serves 6.

Leftover chiles verdes, chili, taco fillings , and, of course, any of the chicken enchilada fillings, are great fillers for chimichangas, especially for last minute preparation. For vegetarians, try rajas poblano.

174

Taquitos or Flautas

Prepare either ground beef or chicken filling. Soften
corn tortillas in hot oil. Place the filling in the
middle of the tortilla and roll the tortilla and
secure the flap with a tooth pick. Place ½ inch
of oil in a skillet, heat over medium heat and fry
until golden and crisp (about 2 minutes). Drain
these well, tilting slightly so the oil runs out.
Remove toothpick or at least warn your guests.
Serve the Taquitos on a bed of shredded lettuce,
topped with a generous helping of guacamole and
sour cream. Sprinkle with chopped onion.

*The thinner the tortilla, the crispier it will get. It is possible
to get tortillas in varying thicknesses. Try the local restaurants as a
source, or there may be a tortilla factory close by.*

Grilled Fish Tacos

1½ pounds firm white fish (cod, catfish, halibut, sea bass or mahi mahi)

Seasoning For Fish:

4   tablespoons chili powder
½   teaspoon salt
½   teaspoon garlic powder
2   teaspoons cumin
½   teaspoon brown sugar

Rub fish with seasoning and grill over hot coals until firm. Cut into pieces for serving in warm tortillas. Serve with:

Chipotle Cream Sauce:

1   cup sour cream
2   tablespoons mayonnaise
2-3 chipotle peppers in adobo sauce, seeded
1   tablespoon or more adobo sauce

Blend ingredients together.

Cabbage:

3-4 cups chopped cabbage
¼   cup chopped cilantro
1   tablespoons lime juice
*   salt & pepper*

Combine cabbage, cilantro with lime juice, salt & pepper.

12 to 24 corn tortillas
fresh lime wedges
fresh picante sauce

Place tortillas between damp dish cloths and steam in
    microwave oven 2 to 3 minutes. Double the tor-
    tillas when filling (two together). Place one piece
    of fish inside cradled tortillas. Add cabbage and
    fresh picante sauce. (see Index) Top with Chipo-
    tle Cream Sauce. Serves 4.

Fish Tacos, Taco Stand Style

1   *pound fish, (cod, catfish or halibut)*

Beer Batter:
1 cup flour
1 cup beer
½ teaspoon salt
1 cup vegetable oil for frying

3   *cups shredded cabbage*
     fresh tomato salsa
     lime wedges
¾   *cup mayonnaise*
2   *tablespoons water*
12   *corn tortillas*

Skin and bone fish and cut into 6 rectangular pieces, or use fillets. Pat dry. Combine flour, beer and ½ teaspoon salt to make batter. Dip fish pieces in batter. Heat oil to approximately 350º in an 8 inch skillet. Add fish a few pieces at a time and fry until golden, about 2 minutes. Drain and keep warm in a 200º oven. Place tortillas between damp dish cloths and steam in microwave oven 2 to 3 minutes. Combine mayonnaise with water to thin for a sauce. Double the tortillas when filling. Place one piece of fish inside cradled tortillas. Add cabbage, mayonnaise and salsa. Finish with a squeeze of lime. Serves 6.

Circle the fish with tin foil to hold together while eating.

Shrimp en Escabeche

Sauce:

2	tablespoons vinegar
2	tablespoons chili powder
1	cup water
4	cloves garlic, finely minced
2	large onions, chopped
1	teaspoon oregano
1	8 ounce can tomato sauce
2	bay leaves
1	16 ounce can tomatoes or 2 cups ripe, peeled, chopped tomatoes

Boil vinegar, chili powder and water together for 10 minutes. Add remaining ingredients and simmer 15 to 20 minutes. Serves 6 to 8.

Shrimp:

4	quarts water
1	tablespoon salt
1	lemon, thinly sliced
3	large ribs of celery with leaves
3	pounds raw, unpeeled shrimp

Peel and de-vein shrimp. Bring water, with salt, lemon and celery to a rolling boil. Add the peeled shrimp. Allow water to return to boil, and cook for 3 to 4 minutes. Taste for doneness after three minutes. Smaller shrimp cook faster than large shrimp ... vary cooking time to match size, continue tasting until done. Do not overcook! Add shrimp to sauce, salt to taste. Serve over hot steamy rice.

Salpicón

8	pounds top sirloin roast
2	cloves garlic
2	bay leaves
1	tablespoon black peppercorns
5-6	dried red chiles or 2 tablespoons crushed, dried red chiles, available at spice counter of supermarket
1	16 ounce can tomatoes
1	cup chopped fresh cilantro, divided
	salt & pepper to taste
8	ounces Italian Salad Dressing (see below)
1½	cups chopped green chiles or 4 fresh roasted poblanos
½	pound Monterey Jack cheese, cut into 1/2 inch squares
2	avocados, peeled and sliced
1	cup fresh parsley
1	medium red onion, thinly sliced

Place beef in a large pot. Cover with water and add garlic, bay leaves, peppercorns, red chiles, tomatoes, ½ cup of cilantro and about a tablespoon of salt. Bring to a boil and then simmer for 5 hours. Remove meat and cool. Cut into pieces roughly 2 inches square, then shred pieces by hand. Place in a 9" by 11" baking dish and cover with salad dressing. Marinate overnight. Top beef with chopped green chiles and cheese squares. Then decorate with avocado slices and sprinkle on remaining cilantro and chopped parsley. Bake at 325° for 20 to 30 minutes, until meat is heated through. Also may be served cold. Serve with Italian Dressing or Lime Chipotle Dressing. Serves 16 to 20.

Italian Dressing:

Combine:

6   ounces oil
2   ounces vinegar
½   teaspoon dried oregano
½   teaspoon basil
    salt & pepper

Lime Chipotle Dressing:

Combine:

½   cup fresh lime juice
3   tablespoons white wine vinegar
3   cloves garlic, pressed
5   chipotle peppers in adobo sauce, chopped and seeded
2   tablespoons adobo sauce.

Cold Salpicón

Marinate the cooked beef in either dressing in the refrigerator for several hours or overnight. Before serving, stir in the onion slices, cheese cubes and chiles Serve on a bed of lettuce and garnish with slices of avocados and tomatoes.

Fajitas

Fajitas (fa HEE tahs) are basically thin slices of marinated, grilled skirt steak topped with a sauce or several condiments and wrapped in a warm flour tortilla. Skirt steak, however, is not readily available in all areas of the country; flank steak is a good substitute. Some suggestions for condiments to serve with Fajitas are salsa or picante sauce, grilled or sauéed onions, Pico de Gallo, chopped tomatoes, chopped lettuce, sour cream, shredded cheese, guacamole or sliced avocado. Use your imagination! Fajitas, once filled are rolled and eaten with your hands. (Serving sizes for Beef or Chicken Fajitas – allow approximately ⅓ pound beef per person and one small boneless breast of chicken per person.) Serves 6.

1½   pounds skirt steak (or flank steak)
½   cup fresh lime juice
3–4   cloves garlic, minced
¼   cup olive oil
1   teaspoon salt
½   teaspoon pepper
6   8-inch flour tortillas

If using skirt steak, make sure that the membrane surrounding the steak has been cut away. Cut the steak in 3 to 4 inch pieces or if using flank steak, leave in one piece. Marinate 4 to 6 hours at room temperature. Grill steak over a hot charcoal and mesquite fire 4 to 5 minutes per side or until desired degree of doneness. Slice steak thinly across the grain. Tightly wrap flour tortillas in foil. Heat at 350° for 15 minutes. Place sliced steak in warm tortillas. Add condiments and roll up.

Chicken Fajitas

1½ to 2 pounds boneless chicken breasts
¼ cup fresh lime juice
¼ cup tequila
¼ cup olive oil
2 cloves garlic, minced
1 teaspoon salt
½ teaspoon pepper

Combine the lime juice,
tequila, olive oil, garlic, salt & pepper. Marinate
chicken breasts 4 to 6 hours in the refrigerator.
Grill over a charcoal and mesquite fire for 8 to 10
minutes per side. Slice in ½ inch strips. Serve in
warm flour tortillas with condiments. Serves 6.

*Another very good marinade for Fajitas is ½ cup papaya
juice and ½ cup vodka. Marinate the chicken or the steak overnight. Pour off the marinade and make a new one of 3 cloves garlic,
minced, 1½ cups beer, ¼ cup olive oil and salt & pepper. Marinate 4
or 5 hours at room temperature and grill.*

A note about mesquite - mesquite is a very hard, fragrant wood that imparts a delicious flavor to
grilled meats. It's generally available commercially
in three forms - chips, chunks and charcoal. Chips
or chunks are simply added to a reqular charcoal
fire shortly before grilling. However, when using
mesquite charcoal only, you should keep in mind
that it burns hotter than normal charcoal briquets.

Chiles Verdes con Carne

2	pounds lean stew beef cut into 1 inch cubes
1	teaspoon salt
1-2	cups beef stock
1	cup chopped onion
1	16 ounce can tomatoes
7	4 ounce cans chopped green chiles
1	clove garlic, chopped

Brown the beef in 1 tablespoon hot oil in a large heavy pot. Add the remaining ingredients and simmer for about 2 hours or until the beef is tender. Sometimes it is necessary to add a little more stock if the stew looks dry. Serve with or over pinto beans and/or rice. Serves 6.

A good make-ahead buffet supper dish. Freezes well.

Carnitas

4	pounds pork shoulder or country style ribs
1	can chicken broth
	water
2	cloves garlic, sliced
2	medium onions, chopped
½	teaspoon ground cumin
½	teaspoon coriander
1	teaspoon salt

Place pork in deep pan and cover with chicken broth and additional water. Add remaining ingredients. Bring to a boil, reduce heat to a simmer. Cover. Cook 2 to 3 hours or until meat is very tender. Drain. Place in a shallow pan and roast at 350° until meat is browned and crispy – about 45 to 60 minutes. Cut into cubes for an appetizer and serve with guacamole or shred and use for tacos, burritos or taquitos.

Leftover PorkRoast:

Shred and place on cookie sheet. Sprinkle with chopped garlic and with lime juice. Add salt & pepper. Roast at 400° until browned and crispy. Serves 8.

Chilaquiles

1 ½ pounds fresh tomatoes
1   large onion, chopped
2   garlic cloves, peeled
6   jalapeño or serrano peppers (or more)
12   corn tortillas
½   cup Monterey Jack cheese, grated
      vegetable oil
      salt & pepper

Broil tomatoes, onions, garlic and peppers until
    browned on all sides, about 5 minutes. Cool and
    then peel tomatoes and peppers and remove their
    seeds. Purée this mixture in a blender or food
    processor, still leaving a few chunks. Cut tortillas
    into ½ inch strips and fry in small batches. Drain.
    Using 2 to 3 tablespoons of oil, sauté tomato
    mixture over medium heat. Add the tortilla strips,
    salt & pepper. Heat for five minutes then sprinkle
    with cheese and serve. Serves 6.

Wow! this dish can pack some heat!

Chilaquiles con Tomatillos

1   *10 ounce can tomatoes with green chiles (drain and save the juice)*
2   *16 ounce cans tomatillos, drained*
1   *clove garlic, crushed*
1   *large onion, chopped*
½   *teaspoon cumin (optional)*
1½ *teaspoons salt (or to taste)*
1½-2 *cups sour cream*
2   *dozen tortillas*
¾   *pound Monterey Jack cheese, grated*
3   *cups cooked chopped or shredded chicken (seasoned with some tomato liquid and ½ cup sour cream)*

Make the green tomato sauce by putting the first six ingredients into a blender or food processor. Blend briefly until mixed well but still a little lumpy. Simmer in a saucepan about 30 minutes. Cool slightly and add sour cream. In a 9" by 13" pan, layer stale, leftover or fresh tortillas (crisp or soft) with cheese and chicken and sauce. Save a little cheese to sprinkle over top. Bake at 325° for 30 minutes.

If you have a little leftover ham, chorizo or beef, these may also be added or substituted for the chicken. Chilaquiles in Southern Mexico is known as "old clothes." This is a dish to improvise with whatever one has. Some like to add another cup of sour cream, thinned with chicken broth and tomato juice. The possibilities are endless! Prepare several hours ahead if convenient. If sour cream is too fattening, try substituting puréed cottage cheese.

Chilaquiles con Pollo

1 *chicken, cooked and deboned (see 'How to Cook a Chicken')*
2 *large onions, chopped*
3 *cloves garlic, chopped*
½ *cup oil*
2 *10 ounce cans tomatoes and green chiles, undrained*
1 *16 ounce can tomatoes, undrained*
1 *tablespoon coriander*
   salt to taste
24 *corn tortillas*
2 *pounds Monterey Jack cheese, grated*
2 *cups sour cream*

Sauté onion and garlic in oil until transparent. Add all cans of tomatoes, coriander, and salt. Simmer 10 to 15 minutes. Cut tortillas into fourths. In another skillet dip tortillas into the hot oil until soft (a minute or less). Drain on paper towels. In a large casserole layer tortillas, sauce, chicken, and cheese. Bake at 350° for 20 to 30 minutes or until bubbly. Serve with a dish of sour cream to the side of the casserole dish. This may be prepared in advance and refrigerated or frozen. Serves 8 to 10.

Arroz con Pollo
(Good ol' Chicken and Rice)

1	*frying chicken, cut into serving pieces or 6 chicken breasts*
½	*cup oil*
½	*cup chopped onion*
1	*cup uncooked rice*
¼	*cup chopped green green pepper*
1	*clove garlic, minced*
½	*cup water*
1	*28 ounce can tomatoes, undrained juice of ½ lime*
1	*teaspoon salt*
½	*teaspoon cumin*
1	*teaspoon chili powder*
½	*teaspoon dried sweet basil or 1 tablespoon fresh sweet basil, chopped*
¼	*teaspoon oregano*

In a heavy skillet, with a tight fitting cover, brown chicken lightly in the oil. Remove chicken from pan and set aside. Sauté onion and pepper until just golden brown. Remove onion and pepper with slotted spoon and set aside. Sauté the rice until golden, stirring frequently. Return onion, pepper, garlic, tomatoes, water, salt and seasonings and bring to a boil. Add the browned chicken, cover tightly and simmer for 30 minutes or until chicken is tender. This dish may also be cooked in the oven in a heavy casserole after browning steps on top of stove. Bake 45 minutes in 325° oven. Garnish with parsley and pimientos for color.

Easy to prepare ahead of time for reheating. Children love this dish!

King Ranch Chicken Casserole

4	*cups cooked chicken*
1	*10¾ ounce can cream of chicken soup*
1	*10¾ ounce can cream of mushroom soup*
1½	*cups chicken broth*
1	*10 ounce can tomatoes and green chiles*
12	*corn tortillas, cut into wedges*
1	*medium onion, chopped*
1	*green pepper, chopped*
2	*cups grated Cheddar cheese*

Combine all the ingredients together except for 1 cup of the grated cheese. Pour mixture into a greased 9" by 13" baking dish and cover with the remaining cheese. Bake at 350º for one hour. Can be made several days ahead. Bake and serve! Perfect for the PTA or church dinner. Serves 8 to 10.

Vegetables
&
Side Dishes

Black Beans

1   pound package of black turtle beans
6   cups water
1   medium onion
1   large clove of garlic
1   bay leaf
3   slices of bacon or 3 ounces salt pork, diced
2   seeded jalapeno peppers (medium size)
    salt & pepper to taste

Rinse and carefully look through the beans for pebbles. Combine all the ingredients in a 3 quart sauce pan. Bring to a boil and simmer covered for 3 hours or until tender. Stir from time to time to be sure beans do not stick and scorch. Add water to keep beans just covered with liquid. Serves 8 to 10.

The addition of 2 teaspoons of cumin powder gives these beans a new dimension.

Texican Squash

2½   *pounds summer squash (yellow, zucchini, pattypan),*
      cubed or sliced
4   *eggs*
½   *cup milk*
1   *pound Monterey Jack cheese, cubed or grated*
1   *teaspoon salt*
2   *teaspoons baking powder*
3   *tablespoons flour*
½   *cup chopped parsley*
1   *4 ounce can chopped green chiles*
2   *chopped, seeded jalapeños (optional)*
1½ *cups crushed tostados or bread crumbs*

Cook squash in 2 cups water until barely tender, about
7 minutes at a boil. Drain and cool in collander.
Mix eggs, milk, cheese, salt, baking powder, flour,
parsley, and chiles together. Fold into squash.
Butter a baking dish, 9" by 13". Sprinkle bottom
with crushed tostado crumbs, or bread crumbs if
you prefer. Pour in squash mixture. Sprinkle top
with more crumbs. Bake at 350° for 30 minutes.
Serves 8 to 10.

Squash and Hominy Dish

2   *pounds yellow squash or zucchini*
2   *cans hominy, drained*
½   *pound sharp cheese, grated*
2   *or more jalapeno peppers, seeded and chopped*
1½   *cups sour cream*
1   *teaspoon salt*
1   *large onion, chopped*
½   *stick butter*

Cook the squash, onion and butter slowly until tender with ½ cup water in skillet. Add the remaining ingredients, reserving 1 cup of cheese. Pour into a 3 quart casserole and top with the remaining cheese. Sprinkle with leftover crushed tostados or Doritos®. Bake at 325° for 1 hour. Serves 8 to 10.

Refried Beans, Frijoles Refritas

½-1 cup vegetable oil, lard or bacon drippings
1   recipe of pinto beans or black beans

Heat the oil over medium heat in a skillet. Add ¼
    of the beans at a time and mash with a potato
    masher by hand. Continue to mash and stir until
    the oil has been absorbed and the beans are shiny
    in appearance (about 30 minutes). Don't overcook
    or they become too dry. Place these in a casserole
    dish, top with grated Monterey Jack cheese. Serve
    immediately or reheat in a 325° oven for 15 to 20
    minutes when needed.

*For another variation of refried beans, try sautéeing a
medium sliced onion in ½ cup olive oil, cooking until the onion is
translucent. Add 4 minced garlic cloves and 1 recipe of black beans,
leaving whole. Cook over medium heat, stirring continually, for
about 20 to 30 minutes or until the mixture is shiny in appearance.
These are wonderful!*

Pinto Beans, Frijoles

1   *pound package dried pinto beans*
1   *large onion, chopped*
1   *10 ounce can tomatoes and green chiles*
1   *tablespoon salt*
1   *tablespoon sugar*
2   *tablespoons chili powder*
½   *pound of bacon (cut into small pieces and sautéed)*

Wash the beans and pick out rocks. Place in a 2 quart pan and cover beans with 4 cups of water. Soak for a few hours if time permits. Bring to a boil, lower heat, add the other ingredients. Simmer for 4 hours, adding water when needed to keep beans just covered with liquid, stirring occasionally until the beans are soft and the juice is thick. Serves 8 to 10.

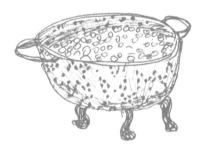

Serve along side a pot of chili.

Mexican Rice

1   cup uncooked rice
½   cup bacon drippings
½   cup chopped onion
1   clove garlic, minced
½   cup chopped green pepper (optional)
3   cups canned tomatoes or V-8® juice or a combination
     of fresh tomatoes and beef broth
     salt

Sauté the rice, onions, garlic and green pepper in the
bacon drippings until the rice is golden. Then add
tomatoes or tomato juice to the rice. Cover and
simmer for 30 minutes. If the rice begins to ap-
pear too dry, add a little water. Serves 6 to 8.

Mexican Green Rice

1   cup long grain white rice
3   tablespoons vegetable oil
1   small onion, chopped
1   clove garlic
2   jalapeño peppers, seeded and chopped
¼   cup fresh cilantro, chopped
1   cup chicken broth or vegetable broth
1   cup water

Sauté onion and rice in vegetable oil until rice is golden. Add chicken broth and water and jalapeño peppers. Cook about 20 minutes until liquid is absorbed. Stir in chopped cilantro before serving.

Jalapeño Rice

1½ cups medium grain white rice
3   cups hot water*
2   tablespoons oil
3   cloves garlic, finely minced
1   small onion, chopped
2   fresh jalapeño peppers, seeded and chopped
    fresh parsley

Sauté onion and garlic in oil until tender. Add the rice and allow it to lightly brown. Add the hot water and jalapeños. Cook 20 to 25 minutes or until all the water has been absorbed. Serve with a sprinkle of fresh chopped parsley.

*1½ cups of chicken broth can be used in place of part of the water for a richer flavor.

Corn and Squash Mexican

2   pounds summer squash, zucchini and yellow crook-
    neck is an attractive combination
1   large onion, chopped
4   ears fresh, sweet corn
4   tablespoons butter
1   cup grated Monterey Jack cheese
1-2 jalapeños, finely chopped

Cook squash in 1 cup water until tender 10 to 15
    minutes. Drain in collander. Sauté onion in but-
    ter. Cut corn from cob. Combine squash, onion,
    corn, jalapeños and cheese. Pour into casserole.
    Bake at 325° for about 30 minutes. Serves 8 to
    10.

Borracho Beans

2   *cups dried pinto beans*
1   *clove garlic, crushed*
2   *teaspoons salt*
4   *slices bacon*
2   *tablespoons bacon drippings*
1   *onion, chopped*
2   *jalapeño peppers*
2   *tomatoes (or one 16 ounce can, drained)*
1   *can beer*

Soak beans in water overnight. Drain and cover with fresh water. Add garlic, salt and bacon. Simmer 2½ hours or until beans are soft. Drain beans and reserve liquid. Heat bacon drippings and saute the onions, peppers and tomatoes until soft. Stir the mixture into beans and simmer 5 minutes. Just before serving, pour beer and as much reserved liquid as desired into beans. Serve hot. Beans can be mashed or 'processed' for refrieds. Serves 8.

Green Chile Hominy Casserole

2   *20 ounce cans white hominy*
2   *4 ounce cans chopped green chiles*
2   *cups sour cream*
2   *cups Monterey Jack cheese, grated*
1   *cup half and half cream*
4   *ounces butter*
     salt & pepper

Drain hominy. Layer half a can of hominy in bottom of a 3 quart casserole. Add ½ cup sour cream, ½ cup cheese and a half can of green chiles. Dot each layer of hominy with butter and sprinkle with salt & pepper. Repeat layers and end with cheese. Just before baking, pour the cream over the casserole to prevent drying out. Bake at 350° for 40 to 50 minutes. Serves 8.

Breads

Flour Tortillas

2 cups flour
½ teaspoon salt
4 tablespoons lard or shortening
½ cup hot water

Mix salt into flour. Cut lard or shortening into flour until uniform crumbly texture is reached. Add hot water gradually, mixing with a fork until dough forms a ball. Knead with your hands on a floured board until dough is elastic and smooth, about 5 minutes. Cover and let dough rest for 10 minutes. Divide dough into 12 golf-ball-sized balls. Roll out one at a time on floured board until approximately 7 inches in diameter. Cook on a hot ungreased griddle 20 to 30 seconds on each side, until spotted and tender. Serve immediately with butter or keep warm in a folded dish towel for up to an hour until serving time. These flour tortillas are so easy and so good - another children's favorite. Flour tortillas may be used for soft tacos, in chilaquiles and even in making enchiladas. Corn tortillas are generally used in this cookbook's recipes, unless otherwise specified.

Soft Tortillas

Masa Harina by Quaker is available in most large
   supermarkets and always in Latin American
   groceries. (Caution! regular cornmeal is not the
   same and will not work!)

2 cups Masa Harina
1 cup water

Mix masa and water with a fork or your hands,
   blending well for a couple minutes. Dough
   should hold together; if not, add a little more
   water, a tablespoon at a time. Shape into 12 to
   16 balls and cover bowl to prevent drying. Allow to stand for 15 to 20 minutes. Flatten each
   ball of dough with tortilla press or rolling pin to
   form 6-inch circles.

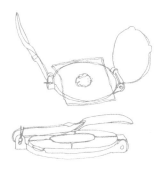

Jalapeño Corn Bread

1½   *cups yellow cornmeal*
3   *teaspoons baking powder*
½   *teaspoon salt*
1   *cup grated Longhorn cheese*
5   *large jalapeños, finely chopped*
3   *eggs, lightly beaten*
½   *cup corn oil*
1   *cup sour cream*
1   *8 ½ ounce can cream style corn or 3 ears fresh corn, cut and scraped from cob*
      optional: ½ cup grated onion

Mix together cornmeal, baking powder and salt. Stir in cheese, onion (optional) and jalapeños. Add eggs, oil, sour cream and corn; mix well. Grease a 9" by 13" pan and pour in the batter. Bake at 400° for 20 to 30 minutes or until a straw comes out clean. Bake Jalapeño Corn Bread batter in greased miniature muffin tins, and cook only 10 to 15 minutes in a 400° oven. Attractive brunch muffins or appetizers!

Sopaipillas

4   *cups flour*
1   *tablespoon shortening*
1   *teaspoon salt*
4   *teaspoons baking powder*
1   *egg, beaten*
1   *cup water*

Sift flour, baking powder and salt. Mix in shortening and knead. Add egg and water to form a stiff dough. Divide dough into four parts and roll out very thin. Then cut into 3 inch squares. Fry in deep hot fat - 350°. The sopaipillas puff up like little pillows! Serve immediately with honey. Makes 3 dozen.

Desserts

Flan

6   eggs, *lightly beaten*
½   cup plus 1 tablespoon sugar
1   teaspoon vanilla
½   teaspoon salt
3   cups milk
½   cup sugar
1   tablespoon water
1   tablespoon rum

Combine the first five ingredients in a food processor
and blend until smooth to make custard. Place ½
cup sugar, water and rum in a skillet over medium
heat. Stir continually until syrupy and brown;
pour into lightly greased 7 ½" by 11" two quart
baking dish. Add the custard. Place the dish in a
hot water bath and bake at 325° for one hour or
until knife inserted in custard comes out clean.
Allow an additional 30 to 45 minutes baking
time if you use a deep flan dish.

Pralines I

2   *cups sugar*
1   *cup brown sugar*
1   *stick butter*
1   *cup evaporated milk*
2   *tablespoons light corn syrup*
4   *cups pecan halves*

Place all the ingredients except the pecans in a heavy
    pan. Heat over medium high heat, stirring, until
    the mixture boils. Continue boiling over low heat
    until the soft ball stage, 238°, on a candy ther-
    mometor is reached (about 30 minutes). Remove
    from heat. Beat until creamy and beginning to
    thicken. Add the pecans and drop by spoonfuls
    onto wax paper. Cool. Store in air tight contain-
    ers.

*For a more intense pecan flavor, spread the pecan halves on
a cookie sheet and roast in a 400° oven for about 5 minutes. Careful
not to burn!*

Pralines II

2   *pounds light brown sugar*
2   *cups granulated white sugar*
¾   *cup light corn syrup*
1   *cup milk*
3   *teaspoons vanilla*
½   *stick butter*
1   *pound pecan halves or pieces*

Cook brown and white sugars, corn syrup and milk to soft ball stage, 240°, without stirring. Remove from heat and add vanilla and butter. Beat by hand until the mixture thickens and drops easily from a spoon. Add the nuts. Drop mixture, a generous tablespoon at a time, onto the waxed paper. Candy will set and harden quickly. If mixture hardens in the pan, add a very small amount of hot water and stir until it softens. Cool and store in an air tight container.

Pralines freeze very well. Store in plastic bags. They thaw quickly and are also delicious to munch on frozen!

Oranges With Wine Sauce

2   cups dry red wine
½   cup sugar
1½   cups boiling water
12   cloves
2   sticks cinnamon
1   tablespoon raisins or currants
1   tangerine, sliced and unpeeled
12   navel oranges

In a pyrex or enamel saucepan, dissolve sugar in the water and add the wine. Add cloves, cinnamon, raisins, tangerine and lemon to the wine mixture and boil slowly until the liquid becomes syrupy, about 35 to 40 minutes. Strain out the spices and fruit with a sieve or slotted spoon. Peel the oranges with a sharp knife removing all the white membrane. Remove segments. Add the orange segments to the wine sauce and chill. Serve garnished with sliced almonds and finely slivered orange peel.

In winter, serve the sauce piping hot with the oranges - so fragrant! For a summer treat use this sauce with fresh, juicy, sliced peaches or pears instead of oranges. Prepare wine sauce ahead and use as needed. It keeps weeks, refrigerated.

Flamed Bananas

6   *slightly green bananas, peeled and halved lengthwise*
½   *cup brown sugar*
⅓   *cup butter*
     cinnamon
½   *cup rum*
¼   *cup liqueur, brandy, Grand Marnier, etc.*

Melt the butter and sugar in a shallow sauce pan. Sauté the cinnamon sprinkled bananas 1 minute on each side. Pour in the rum and liqueur, ignite. If you do not wish to flame, use only ¼ cup rum. Serve immediately with ice cream or/and whipped cream. Scoop up pan juices to pour over all.

One of our frequent dinner guests at large gatherings where everyone brought a dish, was Bob Waldron, a very well known and loved Texan who always brought banana cream pie as his contribution. It was the only thing (he said) that he knew how to make - a little rich for Tex-Mex but greatly appreciated.

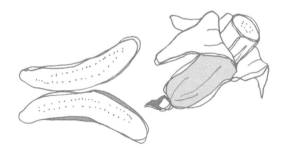

Three Fruit Ice

2   teaspoon unflavored gelatin
¼   cup cold water
1¼   cups sugar
1¼   cups water
1   cup lemon juice
1   cup orange juice
5   bananas, peeled and well mashed
2   egg whites, stiffly beaten

Soften gelatin in the cold water. Boil 1¼ cups water and
   sugar together for 5 minutes. Add softened gelatin
   to the hot syrup. Cool to room temperature and add
   lemon juice, orange juice and bananas. Chill. Add
   stiffly beaten egg whites and freeze in ice trays or in
   an ice cream freezer -hand cranked is best!

A large, colorful bowl of fresh fruit is always a popular dessert.

Strawberry Sorbet

1   *quart fresh strawberries, cleaned and hulled*
½   *cup sugar (adjust amount to sweetness of berries*
1   *tablespoon lemon juice*
½   *cup water*

Using a blender, blend berries into a purée. Add the
sugar, lemon juice and water and blend until all
the ingredients are combined. Pour mixture into
a metal ice cube tray or other similar metal pan.
Freeze several hours or until solid. Break the solid
mixture into chunks and blend to a soft slush
with either a hand mixer or food processor. Place
in a covered container and return to the freezer.
Allow sorbet to sit out a few minutes for easier
serving. 4 Servings

Mango sorbet can easily be made with this recipe. Use
about 4 cups sliced mango, ⅓ cup of sugar, 1½
tablespoons lime juice and ½ cup water.

*The electric ice cream
maker with the frozen remove-
able cylinder makes sorbet making
about a 30 minute process from
start to finish.*

Brownies

1	cup flour
2	cups sugar
¾	cup Hershey's unsweetened cocoa
½	pound butter, melted
4	eggs, beaten
1	teaspoon vanilla
½	cup broken pecans
	pinch of salt

Prepare the pan: Use a 9" by 13" glass pan. Grease with solid shortening and then line the dish with one piece of waxed paper, which has been greased. When waxed paper lining is in place, trim around sides of pan. Combine ingredients to make a batter. Pour batter into prepared pan and bake at 350° for 25 to 30 minutes. Do not over-cook! Use a toothpick to test for doneness. Turn brownies out on a large piece of tin foil, large enough to seal later. Pull the waxed paper off, then place the pan back over brownies and allow to cool. This method locks in moisture, which is the secret to these wonderful brownies. Before serving, cut into squares.

My mother-in-law, Ann Spivy Worley, originally from Bonham, Texas, created these wonderful brownies, praised from Texas to Washington, DC, and many still refer to them as "Ann Worley's brownies".

Mexican Custard Sauce

2   *cups whole milk*
6   *eggs yolks*
⅓   *cup sugar*
¼   *teaspoon salt*
1   *tablespoon vanilla*
1   *cup whipping cream*
1-2 *tablespoons rum (or tequila!)*

Beat egg yolks with sugar and salt. Heat milk but do
not boil. Add gradually to the egg yolk mixture.
Cook in double boiler over boiling water until
custard will coat a spoon. Add vanilla and chill in
refrigerator. Whip cream. When ready to serve,
fold rum and whipped cream into custard and
serve over fresh fruit: oranges, berries, peaches
- cake, brownies, mango mousse.

Vanilla and chocolate are native to Mexico.

Fresh Mangos

Chilled, ripe, fresh mangos with a slice of lime makes
a delightful dessert after a heavy meal.

Mexican Wedding Cookies

1   *stick butter, softened*
1   *cup flour*
¼   *cup confectioners' sugar*
1   *cup pecans, finely chopped*
1   *teaspoon vanilla*
     pinch of salt
     powdered sugar

Combine butter, flour and sugar until well mixed.
Add pecans, vanilla and salt. Roll into balls about
the size of a quarter. Place on ungreased cookie
sheet about 1 inch apart. Bake 20 minutes at
350º. Cool slightly but while still warm, roll in
confectioners' sugar. Store in covered container.

For large, outdoor Tex-Mex gatherings, pass a basket of
fruit popsicles for an easy and refreshing dessert.

Lemon Squares

2   cups flour
½   cup sugar
2   sticks butter
4   eggs, beaten
2   cups sugar
½   cup lemon juice
⅓   cup flour
     grated rind of two lemons
     confectioners' sugar

Make a crust of: flour, sugar and butter. Press in the
bottom and slightly up the sides of an 8" by 11"
glass dish. Bake at 350º for 20 minutes. Make a
filling of: eggs, sugar, lemon juice and rind, and
flour. Pour filling over baked crust. Return to
350º oven for 15 minutes or until set. Cook, then
sprinkle with confectioner's sugar. Cut into small
squares. Refrigerate. Makes 36 squares.

Texas Chocolate Cake

½   *pound butter*
4   *tablespoons cocoa*
1   *cup water*
2   *cups sugar*
2   *cups flour*
1   *teaspoon baking soda*
2   *eggs, beaten*
½   *cup buttermilk*
1   *teaspoon cinnamon*
1   *teaspoon vanilla*
¼   *teaspoon salt*

Melt butter. Add cocoa and water. Bring to a boil.
Combine sugar, flour and soda. Pour in boiled
mixture and combine. Add eggs, buttermilk, cinnamon, vanilla and salt. Pour into a 9" by 13" pan.
Bake at 325° for 30 minutes. Cool cake about 15
minutes and pour freshly made icing over cake.

Icing:

Melt 1 stick butter, 4 tablespoons cocoa and 8 tablespoons milk. Bring to a boil. Pour over one 16
ounce box of confectioners' sugar. Add 1 cup
broken pecans. Pour icing over warm cake.

*May be made a day or two ahead. What a great cake!
Everyone's favorite!*

Index

Index

B

C

E

F

G

O

P

R

T

Please send the following:

_____ copies of It's a Long Way to Guacamole @ $18.95 each $_____

Postage and Handling of $3.50 for the first book $_____

Postage and Handling of $1.00 for each add'l book $_____

Texas residents $1.85 for each book: $_____

Check or credit card: Charge my   Total: $_____

MasterCard ☐   Visa ☐

American Express ☐   Discovery ☐

Account # _____

Expiration date: _____

Signature _____

Mail to:
Newman Marketing
3802 Antelope Trail
Temple, Texas 76504
1-888-458-1229

Name: _____

Address: _____

City _____ State: _____ Zip:_____

Phone: _____ e-mail: _____

Order online: www.annworley.com

Please send the following:

_____ copies of It's a Long Way to Guacamole @ $18.95 each $_____

Postage and Handling of $3.50 for the first book $_____

Postage and Handling of $1.00 for each add'l book $_____

Texas residents $1.85 (sales tax) for each book $_____

Check or credit card: Charge my   Total $_____

MasterCard ☐   Visa ☐

American Express ☐   Discovery ☐

Account # _____

Expiration date: _____

Signature _____

Mail to:
Newman Marketing
3802 Antelope Trail
Temple, Texas 76504
1-888-458-1229

Name: _____

Address: _____

City _____ State: _____ Zip:_____

Phone: _____ e-mail: _____

Order online: www.annworley.com

I'd like to share a favorite recipe: